Having learned to sew at the age of five, Jenny Lord discovered knitting in her early twenties when she could no longer resist the luxury yarns she kept spying in her local haberdashery. This is the book she would have liked to own when she first started knitting.

Jenny lives in London. *Purls of Wisdom* is her first book.

Claire Scully is an artist, photographer and illustrator. Having graduated from Central Saint Martins and the London College of Communications, Claire has worked on projects for the *Guardian*, the *New York Times*, *Wallpaper** magazine and Universal Records and has had her work exhibited in France, Sweden, the US and the UK. Claire draws inspiration from intricate detail and patterns in the natural landscape as well as her love of animals. She lives in North London with two dogs and three cats. Her website is *www.thequietrevolution.co.uk*

PURLS OF WISDOM

Jenny Lord

PENGUIN BOOKS

PENGUIN BOOKS

Published by the Penguin Group
Penguin Books Ltd, 80 Strand, London WC2R 0RL, England
Penguin Group (USA) Inc., 375 Hudson Street, New York, New York 10014, USA
Penguin Group (Canada), 90 Eglinton Avenue East, Suite 700, Toronto, Ontario, Canada M4P 2Y3
(a division of Pearson Penguin Canada Inc.)
Penguin Ireland, 25 St Stephen's Green, Dublin 2, Ireland (a division of Penguin Books Ltd)
Penguin Group (Australia), 250 Camberwell Road,
Camberwell, Victoria 3124, Australia (a division of Pearson Australia Group Pty Ltd)
Penguin Books India Pvt Ltd, 11 Community Centre,
Panchsheel Park, New Delhi – 110 017, India
Penguin Group (NZ), 67 Apollo Drive, Rosedale, North Shore 0632, New Zealand
(a division of Pearson New Zealand Ltd)
Penguin Books (South Africa) (Pty) Ltd, 24 Sturdee Avenue,
Rosebank, Johannesburg 2196, South Africa

Penguin Books Ltd, Registered Offices: 80 Strand, London WC2R 0RL, England

www.penguin.com

First published 2010
1

Set in Futura and Fresco
Printed in China
A CIP catalogue record for this book is available from the British Library

978-1-846-14302-1

For Laurie Sadler, my grandmother and fellow mohair enthusiast

Acknowledgements

Huge thanks to my wonderful editor Nikki Lee for her unflagging enthusiasm, patience and vision and for stepping in to help out with the knitting when it was needed most. To my publisher Helen Conford, for convincing me I could write a book, and to the rest of the Penguin family: Alexis Kirschbaum, Anna Clarkson, Coralie Bickford-Smith, Emma Horton, Mari Yamazaki, Rebecca Lee, Stefanie Posavec and Sam Binnie. Giant thank you to Claire Scully for her beautiful illustrations and photographs and for being so patient while I endlessly contorted my hands and needles trying to demonstrate stitches. Thanks to the talented bloggers and designers around the globe who kindly offered up their patterns – Anna Enge, Debbie Orr, Elly Fales, Heidi Grønvold, Juju Vail, Rebecca Danger, Rose Sharp-Jones, Ruth Bridgeman and Susan Sharp – and to Jane Brocket, Joyce Meader, Laurence Modiano, Lauren O'Farrell, Rachael Matthews and Susan Crawford for offering their time and wisdom. Thanks to Rowan Yarns for their generous yarn donations. For modelling, thank you Laura Wheatley, Oliver Keens, Chris Croissant and teeny Frank Marston. And to Alistair Richardson for the extra photographs and for understanding the pains of being camera shy. To Juliet Annan for her endless support and sage wisdom. Massive thanks to my mum and dad who have always encouraged me to be creative, to my brother Matt for providing welcome distraction and most of all to my sister and best friend Laura for putting up with living in a house full of knitted stuff for so long. And special thanks to Nicky Verber for making the last few months of this marathon more than bearable.

Contents

Introduction

Learning to knit shows us the simple pleasure of turning nothing into something, with what is effectively a couple of twigs and some string. For most of us, using our hands means changing the track on our iPods, typing an email or updating our Facebook status, and we're feeling the need to get back to basics, reconnect with our ancestors and make meaningful decisions about what we clothe ourselves and our babies in: knitting offers the perfect opportunity to do just this. Plus it's fun, relaxing, gives you an excuse to watch crap telly and allows you to connect with a worldwide community of like-minded people. High-profile and Hollywood knitters have helped to prompt a complete change of attitude and knitting is no longer relegated to the happily retired. New yarn shops are cropping up all over the country, haberdasheries are reporting year-on-year increases in sales of yarn, the internet is crawling with bloggers waxing lyrical about their love affair with knitting, and newspapers and magazines are crammed with references to the seemingly baffling resurgence of the craft.

So welcome to the wonderful world of The Knit. You've just taken your first step to joining a global revolution.

Anyone Can Knit

And that's a fact, unless of course you have no fingers (and even then that isn't much of an excuse). Never considered yourself a 'creative person'? No worries – you don't need to be super-skilled or even particularly imaginative to start knitting; at the risk of getting all Jamie Oliver on your ass, with a little patience (and this book) anyone can create a simple but beautiful and professional-looking bramble stitch scarf in an evening or two. As Elizabeth Zimmermann, knitting hero to many, famously said: 'Really all you need to become a good knitter are wool, needles, hands, and slightly below-average intelligence.'

The key is to start small: don't get overexcited and embark on a huge, complicated project that will take every evening for three months to complete. I'm the world's number-one fan of little projects that are quick to make – scarves, hats, wristwarmers and ties – and favour these any day over big projects that take up too much time and put too much pressure on my purse. I have never had a burning desire to knit my own jumpers; it's expensive and time-consuming, and the risk of ending up with something you only want to wear because you're all too aware of the number of evenings it took to make is high. Instead, make a lacy scarf for your mum, or a handsome cushion for your friend's new flat.

This book is a way of sharing with intrepid beginners my pearls of knitting wisdom. I will teach you, without inducing anger or tears, everything you need to know to knit the small stuff and beyond. The patterns in Part Four are categorized by difficulty, from the blissfully simple to the satisfyingly more advanced; but once you've knitted yourself a scarf or two, every pattern in the book will be achievable.

Knitting for Giving

Questioned about the yarn and needles that were accompanying her on every film set, Julia Roberts told one interviewer: 'It's just great to make things. To have a pile of yarn and make it into something.' And goddamn, the woman is right: But that sense of satisfaction shoots right up the scale when you give your creations away. I will never tire of the 'Oh my God, you *made* this?' shriek that comes with giving my knitted wares as gifts, and I can guarantee you won't either. Got a friend who's just had a baby and you'd rather not buy her something generic from Baby Gap? Knit her some tiny booties that she can treasure for ever as 'baby's first shoes' (see p. 152). Got a friend who is seriously fussy and likes plain but high-quality things? Rustle up a simple but luxurious scarf (see p. 130). Your friends are getting married and you don't think the gravy separator on their wedding list is quite the thoughtful and romantic gift you had in mind? Knit them a gorgeous cushion for their bed that can be passed down generations (see p. 164). Down with endless scented candles – give gifts you *know* your friends and family will love because you know them best and can create something, with love, exactly to their taste.

The patterns in this book were all designed to be gifts – for girls, boys, babies and couples. Simple but sophisticated, they can all be easily customized using different yarns, colours and stitch patterns to create the perfect presents for your favourite people. And you'll more than likely want to knit a few things for yourself too.

But before we get to the patterns, prepare yourself for a whirlwind tour of the history of knitting. Understand that, when you knit, you engage in a craft that originated before the twelfth century, a craft that underwent a variety of political, social and cultural changes to become the globally popular activity it is today. Then you will learn everything you need to know about yarn and needles to get you started, and most importantly, through the best illustrations and my trusty beginner's tips, how to actually get down and knit. Once you've mastered the art of knit and purl and have had a go at some of the patterns in this book, I will show you where to find the best yarn, needles and patterns and what else you can do with your new obsession besides sitting on the sofa with your latest project. This book will be your knitting encyclopaedia.

Handmade? Hell, yes!

Quality trumps quantity every time. But of course quality can be costly, and this is where knitting really starts to rock: you can make the most beautiful things with the most luxurious of yarns for the fraction of the price of shop-bought products. It's like that old parable: give a girl £100 and she can buy one beautiful cashmere scarf; give her a pair of knitting needles and £100 worth of cashmere yarn and she can knit beautiful scarves for all her friends and family.

THE HISTORY OF KNITTING

The History of Knitting

We have no idea who first came up with the inspired idea to knit and purl. It's not like anyone thought to preserve the event for posterity – it's hard to imagine whichever genius it was turning to her husband and saying, 'Darling, look what I just made with these twigs and this string,' and her partner replying supportively, 'OMGWTF? This is going to be huge! Let me just make a little note of the date on this scroll here …' But luckily enough, we do know where knitting originated from.

Several museum collections (including the Louvre in Paris and the Victoria and Albert in London) possess some fourth- and fifth-century socks made of what looks like knitted fabric. These 'Coptic socks' – oddly modern-looking things with a built-in division for the big toe (presumably to accommodate the thong of a sandal) – originate from pre-Islamic Egypt and have been worked in the round (which means knitting on four or five needles in a spiral to form a tube) from the toe up. Unfortunately, their structures are difficult to interpret and experts have been having some fairly nasty squabbles over the years about whether these are true knitted pieces or were actually produced by a different technique called naalbinding, which creates a similar appearance. Let them argue, I say.

The earliest knitted pieces came to us from Islamic Egypt, sometime before the twelfth century.

The earliest knitted pieces – fragments of cotton socks with intricate blue and white stitch patterns, some with very impressive Arabic script-ing – that were, hand on heart, created using the knitting technique as we now know it, come to us from Islamic Egypt, some time before the twelfth century. From Egypt, it is likely that knitting travelled to Spain via Mediterranean trade routes and then into the rest of Europe – a few fourteenth-century paintings of the Madonna and Child from both Italy and Germany show Mary knitting (and in the round, no less). However, because weaving was such an established trade and needles were not easy to make (the production of steel rods required a high level of skill from a whitesmith; although this doesn't really seem like much of an excuse to me – hello, *twigs*?), it wasn't until the sixteenth century that knitting really came to the fore. Previously reserved for making specialist items like liturgical gloves, pillows and relic purses (I love the idea that precious things must always be kept in knitted purses), now the very wealthy were wearing knitted caps and stockings. The first knitting guild, set up to control the manufacture and market for knitted goods, was formed in 1527 in France; only men were admitted* and it took six years for students to become master knitters. At the end of this six-year period, each knitter was required to submit his knitted creations – an intricate carpet, a shirt, a beret and a pair of socks – to be examined by the master craftsman. If his work was considered to be at all slapdash or shoddy, he might well have been heavily fined or expelled from the guild. Brutal.

During the reign of Henry VIII (1509–47), the Spanish were busy knitting delicate silk stockings which were the envy of the Courts of Europe. Always one for being ahead of the sartorial game, the king covered his portly calves exclusively in these luxury stockings while his minions had to suffer the coarse cloth stockings of the day. Some years later, Queen Elizabeth's silk woman (where is *my* silk woman?), Mrs Montague, copied a pair of fancy imported stockings based on a lacy French design as a gift for the queen. The queen was so delighted with her gift – hand-knitted silk stockings were probably equivalent to a Ferrari in today's present-giving stakes – that she declared: 'I like silk stockings so well, because they are pleasant, fine and delicate, that henceforth I will wear no more cloth stockings.' What Her Royal Highness wanted she bloody well got and so, slowly but surely, a hosiery trade emerged to meet the demands of the queen and all her wealthy friends.** The rapid growth of stocking knitting during Elizabeth's reign (1558–1603) led to the opening of the first schools for teaching knitting and before too long it became an established feature of English life and an important source of income for the working classes.

....

* It wasn't until knitting became a domestic pursuit that women really took up the sticks; when knitting was a trade and considered 'proper' work, it was the men who ruled the roost.

** And this trade was to prove long-lived and lucrative – by the end of the seventeenth century, as many as two million pairs of stockings had been exported from Britain to other parts of Europe.

The first knitting guild, set up to control the manufacture and market for knitted goods, was formed in 1527 in France; only men were admitted and it took six years for students to become master knitters.

All was going swimmingly for knitting and in 1589, William Lee, a young clergyman from Nottinghamshire, invented the first 'knitting frame'. William was sick of his wife's obsession with knitting stockings; she was paying more attention to her knitting than she was to her husband. Desperate to rectify this dire situation, William came up with a mechanical knitting machine, thus leaving his wife free to fulfil her marital duties of care. Knowing of Queen Elizabeth's partiality for knitted silk stockings, William was eager to seek her patronage. But the queen didn't give him quite the encouragement he was expecting. She was too busy congratulating herself on her Armada victory to pay any real attention to William's little invention and dismissed it on the grounds that it would deprive many skilled hand-knitters of their employment. Undeterred, William packed up his machine and moved to France, where he gained the support of Henry IV. But no sooner had the king given over his patent, he went and got himself executed, putting William's mission to bring down the hand-knitting industry on hold once again. Rather tragically, William Lee died penniless without ever knowing how important his invention was to become (he would have recognized the knitting frames that were used right up until the early twentieth century as based on his own design). Upon his death, William's brother James picked up the baton and returned to England to show off the enhanced models he had worked on with his brother. Although interest in this newfangled way of knitting fabric was kindled, the development of machine-knitting was slow – working away on these rudimentary frames was only fractionally faster than knitting by hand – and made little impact on the hand-knitting industry.

While framework knitting gained some momentum during the years of the Restoration, it wasn't until the dawn of the Industrial Revolution in the late eighteenth century that mass production of cloth shifted to factories and hand-knitting began to lose in the popularity stakes. By the nineteenth century, hand-knitting was no longer a profitable activity and in very real danger of becoming extinct. Only a few isolated groups of people kept the craft alive. In fishing villages along the coastline of England, women knitted sweaters for their fishermen husbands. Each port had its own sweater design (a bit like a football shirt) and you could determine which village a particular fisherman was from by the complicated pattern of cables and bobbles on his sweater. Morbidly, this was a rather useful way of identifying a fisherman should he come to an untimely end

In fishing villages along the coastline of England, each port had its own sweater design and you could determine which village a particular fisherman was from by the complicated pattern of cables and bobbles on his sweater.

at sea. Women would knit their husbands-to-be the traditional sweater of his village to wear on his wedding day, and so they were known as bridal shirts. So romantic! The 'jersey' and 'gansey' (a word which originates from 'Guernsey') jumper styles come from the Channel Islands of the same names. Similarly, the women on Fair Isle, a tiny island north of Scotland, that plays a starring role in the BBC Radio 4 shipping forecast, kept the tradition going through the rise of the machines by developing a complicated technique of working intricate designs (often with sacred meanings) with multiple strands of yarn in different colours which we now call Fair Isle knitting.

Although this was a dark age for hand-knitting, it is interesting to note that the first commercially printed knitting pattern appeared in 1817. The booklet, which consisted of various patterns for socks and stockings, was issued to the National Girls' Schools in order that schoolgirls might learn a profession. It's a very bizarre-looking thing (I have been lucky enough to see it) with patterns that take the form of a series of questions and answers.

Hand-knitting re-entered English life in a big way as a fashionable drawing-room pastime for Victorian ladies of leisure, who devoted their afternoons to handicrafts. And this time, it was here to stay. The first real knitting books were published and printed in large numbers. These books were expensive to buy and the patterns were far from utilitarian: as you might well expect, upper-class Victorian ladies didn't bother themselves with knitting heavy jumpers and underwear but put their dainty fingers to work creating fanciful things like doilies, tea cosies, shawls and bits of fancy lacework.

Victorian ladies put their dainty fingers to work creating fanciful things like doilies, tea cosies, shawls and bits of fancy lacework.

Wartime knitting

It was during the Crimean War that the term 'cardigan' first came into use, named after the Earl of Cardigan, who led the Charge of the Light Brigade and famously wore a knitted vest under his uniform to combat the cold Crimean winter.

During periods of war, the popularity of knitting soared: the Crimean War (1853–6) was the first in which there was a real drive for British women to knit for their army overseas. A book of 'winter comforts' was published, with patterns for blankets, mufflers, gloves, socks, helmets and other necessities for the troops. So urgent and continuous was the need for socks, men also knitted on the frontline. It was during the Crimean War that the term 'cardigan' first came into use, named after the Earl of Cardigan, who led the Charge of the Light Brigade and famously wore a knitted vest under his uniform to combat the cold Crimean winter. The earl may have been a hopeless rake who, following a misinterpreted order, led many of his men to their deaths, but we can thank him for giving a name to the button-down woollen jackets we now call cardigans. Strangely enough, Lord Raglan, the chap who issued the ambiguous instruction, is also important in the history of knitting. Some years before, Raglan had his right arm amputated after sustaining an injury during the Battle of Waterloo and his tailor designed for him a special coat with a diagonal sleeve that would be easier to put on. The classic 'raglan' sweater shape is thus named after Lord Raglan.

During the Boer War of 1899–1902, knitting for the troops again became popular. Patterns for socks, hats, helmets and cholera belts (strips of knitted fabric that were wrapped around the middle to keep the kidneys warm) were widely available, along with pamphlets of patterns for 'hospital comforts' like knee-caps and heel-less socks.

But it wasn't until the First World War that knitting really became a craze. Eager to do their bit for the war effort, women all over the country (and schoolchildren too) knitted socks, scarves and balaclavas for the troops, and camouflage colours were by now standard issue.* Up until this time, military garments had usually been issued in bright colours with the aim of both daunting the enemy and allowing easy identification through the

* The word 'khaki' originates from the Urdu word for dust and described the muddy colour that the British military in India dyed their uniforms after numerous casualties rendered their white hot-weather togs impossible to maintain. Gruesome.

'fog of war'. (I sometimes picture those poor soldiers fighting the Crimean War dressed from head to toe in hot pink.)

Women at this time were so taken with the craft, knitting on trains, in restaurants and at the theatre, that the Church even made a special concession to allow women to knit during services. Knitting became a national mania and 'comforts committees' were set up to rally women together to co-ordinate their knitting for the troops.*

By the time the war ended, women were reluctant to surrender their obsession and so, inspired by the high-fashion knitted designs of Elsa Schiaparelli and Coco Chanel, a trend for knitting jumpers and bathing suits came to dominate the 1920s. Fair Isle knitting was fashionable at this time too, after the Prince of Wales (later to become King Edward VIII) was photographed playing golf in a particularly natty Fair Isle sweater. The first knitting magazines (*Good Needlework*, *Stitchcraft* and *The Needle Woman*) arrived in the 1930s and women's weekly magazines often featured knitting patterns with designs modelled by celebrities of the day.**

So it follows that the Second World War saw women picking up the sticks again to knit for their boys abroad. Although wool was in short supply, the Ministry of Information's 'Make Do and Mend' booklet encouraged women to unpick old woollen garments in order to recycle the yarn and provided advice on how to make yarn go further with instructions for darning and mending woollens. While a lot of their time was devoted to knitting for the war effort, women also made things for themselves – knitted hats, boleros, sweaters and cardigans were a great way to accessorize and bring a little variation to their limited wardrobes. Wool was rationed but the yarn required to make more than one sweater could be obtained for the same number of coupons needed for a ready-made machine-knit version. Knitting was an important and established part of society and so, naturally enough, references began creeping into popular culture. Glenn Miller, the popular American swing musician, entertained the troops with his rather romantic ditty 'Knit One, Purl Two' – a young

*In 1915, the first Women's Institute in Britain was founded in Wales, and no doubt there was a whole lot of knitting going down there too.

** A surprising number of celebrities modelled for knitting patterns early in their careers, including Roger Moore (before his Bond days), who later became known affectionately to Michael Caine as the 'Big Knit'.

Women at this time were so taken with the craft, knitting on trains, in restaurants and at the theatre, that the Church even made a special concession to allow women to knit during services.

Ogden Nash's 1945 poem 'Machinery Doesn't Answer Either, But You Aren't Married to It' tells the story of a man who resorts to talking to himself because his wife is too busy knitting to pay him any attention.

woman sings about knitting a sweater for her sweetheart to keep him warm while he is at war. Ogden Nash's 1945 poem 'Machinery Doesn't Answer Either, But You Aren't Married to It' tells the story of a man who resorts to talking to himself because his wife is too busy knitting to pay him any attention. I'm sure he would have got on fabulously with Rev. William Lee.

Knitting in Postwar Britain

After the Second World War, women were encouraged to get back into the home and reclaim their role as 'domestic goddess'. A range of synthetic yarns arrived; nylon, which was first developed in 1935, along with polyester and acrylic, which both came into commercial production in the 1950s, were extremely popular fibres. Cheap and convenient, these new machine-washable yarns with their wonderful 'wash and wear' quality were welcomed by women desperate to be released from the drudgery of hand-washing and ironing, especially once the electric washing machine became a fixture of the modern British home in the 1950s. While in recent years, rationing had caused knitters to stop their sleeves above the elbow and crop the bodies of jumpers and jackets, 1950s knitwear returned to the extravagance of the 1930s – rounded shoulders, bat-wing sleeves and longer bodies were all the rage.

Norbury believed there was an absolute right and wrong when it came to knitting: 'I was a foolhardy lover who has always been prepared to throw his loyalty and devotion at the feet of Mistress Knitting.'

James Norbury, chief designer for Patons and Baldwins (manufacturers of yarn and patterns, still going strong as Patons), knitwear designer and author of the original *Penguin Knitting Book* (1957), had a huge influence on knitting Britain in the years after the war. Like Elizabeth Zimmermann, Norbury was a popular television personality in the 1950s, here and in the US. Yet *unlike* EZ, Norbury believed there was an absolute right and wrong when it came to knitting: 'I was a foolhardy lover who has always been prepared to throw his loyalty and devotion at the feet of Mistress Knitting.' Saucy stuff.

By the 1960s, the decade of youth culture, styles were skimpier and colours were bolder and brighter. Knitwear was all about the Mary Quant-style mini skirt and figure-hugging sweaters. In 1967, hip young French designer Sonia Rykiel was crowned 'queen of the knits' for her highly fashionable experimental sweater designs.

But as popular as knitting (and high-fashion knitwear) was becoming, two things happened to prompt a gradual decline that would eventually see knitting firmly kicked into the realm of the elderly. Firstly, a little thing called feminism got in the way. With the popularization of American feminist Betty Friedan's 1963 book *The Feminine Mystique*, knitting and other handicrafts became increasingly viewed as symbols of female oppression. Second-wave feminism, concerned with picking up the baton from the suffragettes to fight for social equality for women, had knitting down as synonymous with the submissive housewife who cooked and cleaned by day and knitted and sewed for her husband and children by night. Knitting, and other pursuits that were seen as 'women's work', were thought to subjugate women by restricting them to serving others. Inspired by the activism of Friedan, and later Germaine Greer, women discontented with their lot as second-class citizens began to put down their needles in a bid for liberation, feeling that if knitting was too lowly a task for men then it wasn't something they should be wasting their time with either.

By now, knitting machines were a great deal more sophisticated than William Lee's rudimentary frame, and a machine-knitted jumper could be purchased for the same price as the yarn and pattern required to make it. Although knitting was still a part of life for many women in the 1970s – the fashion for tank tops in sludgy colours and the extraordinary obsession with trying to recreate David Starsky's* chunky-knit, belted and collared cardigan saw to that – it had been firmly set on the path that would eventually lead it to almost disappear from the everyday. Sales of patterns and yarns took a nosedive in the 1980s, when the arrival of 'loadsamoney' culture, yuppies, credit cards and a penchant for power-dressing in designer threads meant that homemade was just too twee to be fashionable. Showing off your money was the name of the game and knitting, which was by then a byword for skint, failed to make the grade. Relegated from a useful skill to just a hobby, by the 1990s knitting had been kicked to the curb, embraced only as a pastime by grandmas.

By the 1990s knitting had been kicked to the curb, embraced only as a pastime by grandmas.

* One half of popular American TV detective duo *Starsky and Hutch*.

The Knit Revolution

After spending the 1990s cast aside by anyone not yet retired, knitting made a major comeback in the first years of the twenty-first century, helped along by a few very special people.

Debbie Stoller realized she had to dispel this crazy idea that knitting was somehow anti-feminist. She embarked on a mission: to 'take back the knit'.

A Yale graduate with a PhD in the psychology of women, co-founder and editor-in-chief of third-wave-feminist popular-culture magazine *Bust*, Debbie Stoller publicly suppressed her love for the craft for years, fearful that it didn't marry well with her feminist beliefs. After all, feminists had forever been declaring that women who spent their time cooking, cleaning, knitting and sewing for their husbands and children were frittering their lives away. But one afternoon in 1999 changed all that for Debbie. On a long train journey across the country, she decided to revisit an unfinished jumper she'd begun knitting years before and – lo and behold! – she had her knitting epiphany: why should she not take pleasure from doing something she loved just because men don't do it too? Surely people who saw knitting as a sign of female oppression were actually striking a blow against the feminist cause by assuming that only the things that men did were worthwhile? Arriving back in New York, her newfound obsession was met with mixed reactions: friends either begged her to pass on her skills to them or couldn't quite believe that she would be interested in knitting. I mean, what the hell was she playing at? How could a feminist possibly see fit to knit? Debbie realized she had to dispel this crazy idea that knitting was somehow anti-feminist. She embarked on a mission: to 'take back the knit' and reclaim the craft for a new generation. So she talked about how much she loved knitting to anyone who would listen, wrote about it (without irony) in her magazine and, gathering together some friends, she organized the first New York City Stitch 'n Bitch group, where men and women could meet and knit (in public – gasp!), share their skills and knowledge and have fun while they were at it. Spreading the love like this was a slow-burner: the idea that knitting was a thing of the past was so deeply ingrained, especially in her feminist circles, that her mission was never going to be an easy one. But she eventually began to notice that she wasn't the only one rediscovering the joys of knitting and rejecting these backward notions of the craft being anti-women. Soon enough it seemed that young people were at it everywhere she looked. These women, who were knitting in bars, on the subway and in coffee shops, in groups and on their own, were reclaiming the craft, not to clothe their husbands and children but to enjoy knitting for themselves.

Across the pond, in 2000, London artist Rachael Matthews – like Debbie – was desperate to give knitting an image makeover. Having learnt to knit when she was eight years old, she felt it was time to do something about the preconceptions so heavily attached to the craft. While Debbie Stoller came at knitting from a feminist angle, Rachael was more concerned with its potential as a political force. With roots in punk and the DIY movement (the anti-consumerist ethic of being self-reliant by doing things yourself), she found that expressing herself by knitting her own clothes was a vital way for her to say she was doing her own thing.

With the aim of seeking out like-minded souls, Rachael and her friend Amy set up Cast Off, a knitting club for boys and girls. Embracing knitting's lack of any elitist element (unlike more conceptual art forms, which can be difficult for the average person on the street to engage with), Cast Off welcomed anyone who had an interest in knitting with open arms, whether they were young, old, man or woman. It started small, just a couple of friends happily knitting and catching up over a few pints in the pub, but with the club's condition to keep things fresh and never meet in the same place twice, more and more people began to join in. And so their crafty club grew.

As an artist, Rachael was concerned with preconceived ideas of what you can and can't do in public spaces, and to challenge these notions, Cast Off began meeting in some very unexpected venues – on the London underground, at the Tate, on an anti-war march, to name a few. They were out there knitting and purling for the world to see and people started paying attention. By 2003, the press couldn't seem to get enough of Cast Off, particularly after the group was thrown out of the posh Savoy Hotel in London by a head waiter who said that knitting was something that should be done at home. Knitting was everywhere and it became *cool*: national newspapers ran articles about the seeming paradox of 'hip young knitters'* and celebrities the world over were

....

* And the headlines were predictably pun-tastic: 'Good Wool Hunting!' said the *Daily Mirror*; 'Zen and the Art of Knitting' was the *Daily Telegraph*'s shot; the *Independent* exclaimed, 'It's a Knit-In!'; and my favourite 'Grandma Sews Best' in *The Times*.

Women knitting in bars, on the subway and in coffee shops, in groups and on their own, were reclaiming the craft, not to clothe their husbands and children but to enjoy knitting for themselves.

coming clean about their secret yarn addictions, from *Sex and the City's* Sarah Jessica Parker to Kate Moss and even Russell Crowe (okay, this last one might have been just a nasty rumour). Over in the states, Debbie Stoller's seminal *Stitch 'n Bitch: The Knitter's Handbook* (2003) sold so many copies that it hit the *New York Times* bestseller list. Up until then, knitting had been a dirty word, dowdy and somehow very uncool, yet this book about knitting was making significant waves among the young and trendy of America. It seemed that finally the efforts of both Debbie and Rachael had paid off. Since then, the number of people coming to the craft for the first time (or picking up their sticks again after years in the closet) has been on a steady increase and, with the help of the internet, knitting really has spread to the masses.

The number of people coming to the craft for the first time (or picking up their sticks again after years in the closet) has been on a steady increase.

But two women, no matter how determined and generally fabulous they are, do not a revolution make. Although Debbie and Rachael waved the flag for the dying craft at a time when it was most needed, they didn't have much control over who might sit up and take notice. Luckily, it just so happened that while knitting was ready and waiting for its major comeback (just like John Travolta pre-*Pulp Fiction*) the world was willing to welcome it back with open arms.

The Craft

For women of our grandmothers' generation, knitting, like sewing, was just something they did. Back in the days before fashion was so disposable, everything was handmade. And I'm talking *everything*. My mother can't remember wearing a single item of clothing as a child that wasn't either sewn or knitted by her mother. And that, rather unfortunately, included her bathing suits.

She herself learnt to knit when she was a tiny child living in deepest darkest Wales. With no television, little spare cash and a distinct lack of brightly coloured plastic crap, my mum and her little sisters kept themselves amused by sewing and knitting. When they were older, they used the skills they had learnt at home and at school* to make their own clothes.

In fact, even during the post-war period, when people had a more generous disposable income, most of the population were still making the majority of their clothes. Without the high-street clothing chains, clothes just weren't available to buy in the way they are now. If you wanted something to wear, you probably had to make it yourself. For women like our mothers and their mothers before them, knitting wasn't about joining a movement or learning a craft; it was only about making clothes, because for most people, if you couldn't make it, you couldn't have it.

Today, knitting isn't so much about the knitwear as about the craft itself. It isn't a skill we all just happen to possess any more; learning to knit requires an active decision. For some of us, this decision is born out of a desire to reclaim the craft under a feminist agenda, for others, it's a politically engaged art form or a way of sticking a finger up to consumerist culture. For me, it started out as another string to add to my crafting bow. I come from a family of people who are good with their hands – my mum can knock up anything on her sewing machine, my dad is a master carpenter who makes the most beautiful furniture, my sister is a talented painter and culinary genius, and my musician brother makes weird electronic boxes that the rest of us can't even begin to understand. So finding knitting has been a most natural step from my love of sewing and textiles. Yet what makes me raise my hands and say, 'Praise be the knit!' is that so many people who are joining this knitting revolution don't have the inbuilt incentive that I do to learn a new handicraft. In our culture of fast, cheap fashion, knitting is not a necessity, so why, why, why, when we have so little time to spare, are so many of us getting out there and choosing to do this?

The reasons are not too difficult to fathom if we look at the world we're living in today. We've invented machines that can do pretty much everything for us; we work in jobs where we rarely get to touch the end product of our efforts; the most exercise our fingers get these days is a keyboard workout. Without meaning to get all Marxist, we are, pretty much, an appendage of the machines we work for and with. *We want to create.* We're tired of being led by the hand to buy the latest fashion

Today, knitting isn't so much about the knitwear as about the craft itself. It isn't a skill we all just happen to possess any more; learning to knit requires an active decision.

....

* My mum and her sister remember knitting and sewing things at school to donate to a local orphanage for Catholic children run by the diocese. They called them 'the bishop's babies', which sounds incredibly dubious if I think about it for too long.

We want to create. *Just as many of us are growing our own vegetables, making our own clothes, learning to cook or making our own furniture, knitting can be seen as part of a larger cultural shift.*

or must-have home accessory; we want our decisions about what to wear to be based on more than just a preference for Primark, Topshop or Selfridges. Just as many of us are growing our own vegetables, making our own clothes, learning to cook or making our own furniture, knitting can be seen as part of a larger cultural shift to embrace our individuality and take the decisions about what we clothe ourselves in, what we put into our bodies, what we surround ourselves with and what we swaddle our babies in back into our own hands.

We want to connect ourselves to our ancestors. Skills like knitting, sewing, cooking and carpentry are no longer passed down through the generations, and that's kind of sad (and annoying when your boyfriend can't even put up a simple shelf). Learning to knit has made me feel closer to my grandmother as I think about how, years ago, she would have sat just like I do (although probably not in front of *The Wire*), knitting up a fluffy little something of an evening.

Learning to knit is an easily achievable goal, no matter what your motivations are. Most people who try to learn to knit have done just that, because unlike playing an instrument or speaking a new language (skills so many of us wistfully toy with the idea of learning but disregard because we don't have the confidence), you aren't required to possess any kind of talent to knit. As Richard Sennett argues in his wonderful book, *The Craftsman* (2008), when it comes to craftwork, 'there is no fixed line between the gifted few and the incompetent mass'. This idea is most applicable to knitting: because anyone can teach themselves to knit in an evening, it is always already in your grasp.

So that's why we're all here today. We saw an easy opportunity to learn a new skill, to get back to basics and to reclaim our individuality, and we grabbed it.

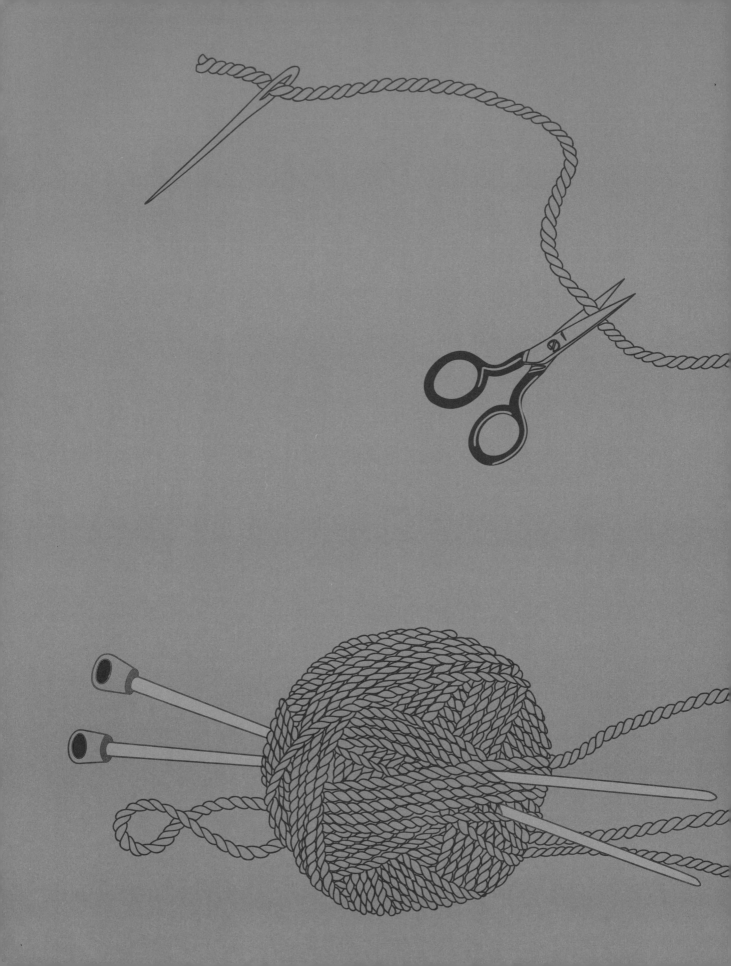

BEFORE YOU START

Choosing Yarn

Shopping for yarn can be a seriously confusing experience. The array of fancy yarns kicking around these days is bewildering and I have almost been reduced to tears on a number of occasions in my local yarn shop trying to decide on the perfect fibre for my latest project. There are two vital factors to consider before you can even begin to think about making your selection: yarn type (its composition, what it's actually made of) and yarn weight (its thickness).

Types of Yarn

Most people call all yarn wool, but wool is only the stuff that comes from sheep and yarn can be made from lots of other things.

Yarn is the term used to describe strands of fibre that have been twisted together to create a continuous length. Most people call all yarn wool, but wool is only the stuff that comes from sheep and yarn can be made from lots of other things. In fact, pretty much anything furry or fibrous can be spun into yarn – even, if you're that way inclined, the fur from your beloved cat.*

Blended yarns combine the unique properties of two or more fibres and can be a great way to add a touch of luxury to a project without you having to shell out for an expensive pure fibre like cashmere. Many of the yarns you'll find in your local yarn shop will be blended, like Rowan Cashcotton, which, as you can probably guess, is a blend of cashmere and cotton.

* I'm being serious – there's an American company who will spin Tabby's fur into yarn if you lovingly collect it off your soft furnishings and send it to them: www.vipfibers.com. Totally sick.

Wool comes from sheep. There are many different breeds of sheep, so there are many different kinds of wool – from the wool of Shetland sheep, which is scratchy but very tough, to merino wool, which is fine, soft, smooth and a joy to knit with. Wool is strong, durable and has the benefit of keeping you warm in winter and cool in summer.

Mohair is a fuzzy yarn spun from the fleece of Angora goats (not to be confused with Angora rabbits, see below). Its softness varies dramatically depending on the age of the goat: kid mohair, which comes from the first and second shearings of goats as young as six months old, is very soft and fine, while adult mohair tends to be a bit coarse. Although it will keep you incredibly warm, adult mohair can be horribly scratchy so it isn't ideal for making things that are to be worn right next to the skin. A mohair scarf is a *bad* idea, a bright turquoise 80s-style batwing cardigan, however, is a *marvellous* idea. Because mohair is so damn fuzzy, it will hide a multitude of sins but its fuzziness also makes it tricky to see individual stitches as you're working, so perhaps save pure mohair projects until you're a little more proficient.

Cashmere is combed from the bellies of the cashmere goats that come from the Himalayas (the goats were originally named after the Kashmir region of India). Cashmere is so soft it really is a joy to behold. But it's as expensive as it is luxurious so don't waste your hard-earned cash knitting it into a knee-length cardigan; use it for smaller projects or try a cashmere yarn blended with another, cheaper fibre.

Alpaca comes from the fleece of alpacas (South American animals that look a bit like llamas). Because it feels so luxurious but isn't too expensive, alpaca is often referred to as the 'poor man's cashmere'. But don't let that put you off: it's smooth, soft and very warm, and an alpaca blend would be perfect for knitting up gloves, scarves and hats.

Angora comes from the coats of Angora rabbits. It's super soft, lightweight, warm and very fluffy but because it's very fine, it has an annoying tendency to shed. Angora will hide mistakes in your work but can be difficult for beginners to knit with because the fluff obscures the stitches. Like cashmere, angora isn't cheap, so it's best to save the pure stuff for smaller projects and use a nice angora blend for the rest.

For the Love of Wool

I must digress at this point and tell you a little more about the fairest yarn of them all: wool. I feel a bit sorry for wool – with all those other chichi fibres to compete with, it seems to have been pushed aside as 'unexciting'. Sure, I understand the unadulterated delectation of pure cashmere and the thrill of hot-pink mohair, but wool is where it's at as far as I'm concerned. When you consider the benefits of wool, it beats those other fancy-pants fibres hands down. Wool can keep you warm or cool you down; it's strong, breathable, absorbent, hypo-allergenic, naturally antibacterial, flame-retardant, renewable, sustainable and biodegradable and has a natural elasticity that allows it to retain its shape. Plus – and this is a little known fact, so pay attention – the finest wool is *softer* than cashmere.

The quality of wool is determined by its fibre diameter, i.e., how fine it is, which is measured in microns. The finer it is, the softer it is. Cashmere is a very soft fibre because it's incredibly fine – usually 13–16 >

microns to be exact, and when you consider that most human hair is around 40–50 microns, the picture becomes clearer. But the fibre from the fleece of the world's most valuable sheep (an Australian breed of Saxon Merino) is even finer at 11.5 microns, which makes it about as soft as any fibre can be. So you see what I mean? Wool totally has the X-factor. 100 per cent wool? It's 100 per cent yes from me. Remember the Woolmark? That classy swirling logo? That little mark guarantees that your cardigan, scarf or ball of yarn has reached certain industry standards. Kind of like an organic certification. It seems bizarre to me, when so many of us are such middle-class bores about ensuring every morsel that passes our lips is certified organic, that we sometimes forget to take care over the quality of the fibres we clothe ourselves in. We should all be paying more attention to that pretty little logo, if only to save ourselves from the evils of 90 per cent acrylic. I breathe a sigh of relief and rest assured I am in the company of quality when I spot the Woolmark and give myself a pat on the back for being such a sensible girl – my mother would be proud.

Silk is spun from silkworm cocoons. It's smooth, light and has an intense jewel-like lustre, but its lack of elasticity can make it a challenging fibre for beginners. Use it to make lightweight things like lacy scarves and shawls or use a silk blend to add a bit of slinky glamour to a project.

Cotton is a plant fibre that is strong, light and absorbent. It's usually machine washable so perfect for making things for babies. While the fluffiness of wool and other furry yarns can hide mistakes in your work, cotton is less stretchy and will highlight every dropped stitch, so perhaps it's not the best yarn to choose for your first project.

Linen comes from the fibres of the flax plant. Linen is a little inflexible and can be a bit stiff but it's stronger than cotton, smooth and cool to wear, which makes it a popular choice for summer clothing. Linen can usually be machine washed and ages beautifully.

Acrylic is a synthetic yarn made by a complicated chemical process that I can't even begin to understand so won't try to explain. It's cheap and machine washable but has a static, stiff quality that makes me itch just to think about. I'd avoid 100 per cent acrylic altogether and go for an acrylic blend to make novelty items like iPod socks.

Your pattern will suggest which yarn is best for you to use but the final decision is of course yours. Lots of beginners find themselves unhappy with the end results of their first projects because the yarn they chose doesn't marry well with the pattern, so when substituting yarns (see p. 38, for more on this), think carefully about the fibre content of your yarn – don't go choosing a scratchy mohair for a scarf or a stiff linen for a hat.

Yarn Weights

As well as differing in fibre content, yarns are also available in different weights. The weight of a yarn describes how thick it is and is usually determined by how many strands (or plies) the yarn is made up of.

2-ply is the thinnest yarn available and the finest, lightest stuff feels like knitting with cobwebs. Usually 2-ply yarn is knitted on big fat needles to create lacy, openwork scarves and shawls but if you've got lots of time and patience, you can use smaller needles to create a professional-looking tight-weave fabric with teeny weeny stitches.

4-ply is roughly double the thickness of 2-ply. Sometimes called 'baby yarn', it is, unsurprisingly, a good weight for making baby clothes because it's lightweight and creates a tight-weave fabric that won't allow little digits to get stuck between stitches. It's also perfect for making socks and you'll find that most of the yarns sold specifically as sock yarn* are 4-ply.

Double-knitting (DK) is a little thicker than 4-ply and is good for making hats, socks, baby clothes and any other project that calls for a fairly tight-weave fabric.

Aran is the most widely available weight and the most frequently used. It's about double the thickness of DK and is great for making scarves, hats, gloves, jumpers and just about anything else you can think of. It's easy to handle and knits up fairly fast, which makes Aran the ideal weight for a beginner.

Chunky is about double the thickness of Aran and will knit up super fast. Chunky yarn is perfect for whipping up last-minute gifts – you can make a chunky scarf or cowl using big needles in an evening.

* A note on sock yarn: although some yarns are specifically labelled 'sock yarn', that doesn't mean they must be used exclusively for knitting socks. Any 4-ply (or slightly thicker) yarn that has been blended with a synthetic fibre could be described as sock yarn. So if you come across a particularly tasty sock yarn and fancy it for a hat, go right ahead.

The Americans use different names to describe yarn weights, which can make things a little tricky when you're shopping on the internet. Here's a handy key:

2-ply = lace
4-ply = fingering
DK = sport
Aran = worsted
Chunky = bulky
Super-chunky = super-bulky

Super-chunky is fat and bulky and the ultimate yarn for a fast knitting fix. It feels a little weird to knit using such massive needles but you'll yield your knitted fabric at an astonishing speed – you can make a fat and snuggly scarf in a matter of hours.

Yarn weight is by no means an exact science and there can be a lot of variation within each of the categories described above. This is why it's important to take the whole picture into consideration when you're thinking of using a different yarn from the one suggested by your pattern – as well as yarn weight, needle size and tension play an important part in determining how your knitted fabric will turn out. See p. 38 for more on substituting yarns.

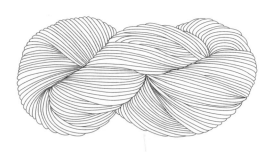

How to Read a Yarn Label

❶ Yarn brand and name: e.g., Rowan Cashsoft. I really love yarn names, especially the more exotic-sounding ones, and think my dream job would be to come up with names for new yarns: 'Oooh! A soft and sensuous merino and mohair blend – I shall call him "Cocoon"!'

❷ Yarn colour and dye lot: yarn colour needs no explanation (you get some fancy names for these too) but I can't stress enough the importance of this funny little code that tells you the dye lot. Yarn is dyed in big batches and every batch will be slightly different in colour from the next. For a one-colour project, you'll want to make sure all those balls have been dyed in the same batch, i.e., they are from the same dye lot. When you're shopping for yarn, it's better to buy too much and end up having to return the unused stuff to the shop than to go back for more and find they no longer have the right dye lot – mixing dye lots can produce some odd-looking stripy patterns in your work.

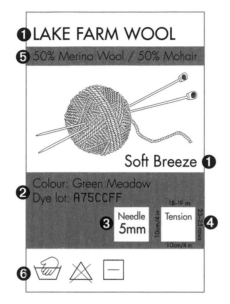

❶ LAKE FARM WOOL

❺ 50% Merino Wool / 50% Mohair

Soft Breeze ❶

Colour: Green Meadow
❷ Dye lot: A75CCFF

❸ Needle **5mm**

Tension

18–19 sts
10cm/4 in
20–25 rows
10cm/4 in **❹**

❻

❸ Needle size: lets you know which size needles you should use with this yarn.

❹ Tension: this little square tells you how many stitches and rows make up a 10cm (4in) square with this particular yarn. Vital information when you're being brave and using a different yarn from the one your pattern calls for.

❺ Yarn content: tells you what the yarn is actually made of, i.e., are we talking bunny, goat, llama-type thing or manmade synthetic?

❻ Washing instructions: does what it says on the tin. Want to throw that gorgeous merino-wool sweater that took you three months to knit in the washing machine? Go ahead, but be prepared for what you pull out of the machine an hour later to be more suitable to clothe a child. Do your friend a favour when you give her those miniature knitted booties for her new baby: wrap them up with a little note letting her know how to wash them.

Yarn labels are *useful things* so don't go throwing them away willy-nilly. If you don't use your whole ball of yarn, make sure you store the leftovers with the label so that when you come to pick it up again you'll know what flavour it is. And if you finish a project and find you are particularly pleased with the results a certain yarn has yielded, staple the yarn label to the pattern for future reference.

Substituting Yarns

There can be a huge amount of variation between yarns in the same weight bracket so there's more to picking a replacement than simply matching the weight.

Once you've moved beyond knitting simple scarves and on to reading patterns, you'll often find that you want to use a different yarn from one suggested by your pattern. There are many reasons for this: maybe the yarn your pattern calls for you to use has been discontinued or it just isn't readily available in the UK. Maybe you're allergic to that particular fibre or perhaps it's a simple matter of the suggested yarn not being available in the knock-out canary yellow your heart is set on. Whatever the reason, you'll find yourself substituting yarns fairly often.

There can be a huge amount of variation between yarns in the same weight bracket so there's more to picking a replacement than simply matching the weight. The Aran-weight yarn in your pattern may be markedly thicker than the Aran-weight yarn you've had your eye on and if you go ahead and knit using the thinner yarn, your project will end up smaller than it's supposed to be. Of course, this doesn't matter massively when you're knitting things that don't need to be a particular size, like scarves or toys or bags, but it can make the world of difference and render something entirely useless when it comes to knitting clothes or hats or gloves.

To find the perfect substitute yarn, you'll need to know a little bit more about the yarn in your pattern. Firstly, you need to pay attention to *tension*. Tension (or gauge, as the Americans call it) describes how many stitches and rows make up a 10cm/4in square of knitted fabric with that particular yarn and the suggested needle size and will give you a more accurate picture of how thick the yarn is. You should search for a yarn that has the same tension (give or take a stitch or row) as the suggested yarn.

Secondly, you need to take needle size into consideration – if the yarn in your pattern calls for size 2.25–3.5mm needles, so must your substitute yarn.

And finally, you need to make sure you buy the right amount of yarn. There's more to this than simply buying the same number of balls of yarn. Yarns come in different lengths – a ball of one type of Aran merino yarn may be 150m long while another Aran merino yarn might come in 200m balls. Check how many metres long one ball of yarn in your pattern is and if it's more than your substitute yarn, buy an extra ball or two.

Winding a Skein into a Ball

The major British yarn companies are usually kind enough to sell us their yarn in neat round balls. For some reason, the Americans (and it's not just them – lots of independent sellers seem to be allergic to balls too) give us the goods in a 'skein' – a giant twisted loop with one end tucked into the other.

Skeins are much prettier to look at than boring old balls but, rather annoyingly, you can't just start knitting with yarn that's wound into a skein: I've tried it (and more than once because I'm an idiot) – the pretty thing very quickly turned into an ugly mess that took hours to untangle. When you buy yarn in a skein, you'll need to wind it into a ball before you can get on and knit. Most independent yarn shops will have a clever foot-operated machine that can do this for you, so do ask in the shop, but if you've bought your yarn over the internet, you'll have to tackle the task yourself. After a great deal of experimentation and a few tears of frustration, I've found the best way to do this is as follows:

1 Untwist the skein and untie the short strands of yarn that are holding the big loop together.

2 Slip the loop over the back of a chair.

3 Locate an end of yarn and wind it around all the fingers on one of your hands (you want to wind it nice and loose otherwise you'll end up stretching and damaging the yarn).

This is quicker (and all the more fun) if you happen to have one of those old-school swivelling office chairs to hand . . .

Looking After Your Yarn

Listen up: *store your yarn sensibly*. I understand that wicker baskets bulging with exquisite balls of yarn look lovely on display, but leaving your yarn in the open-air where evil little moths can freely come and lay their eggs so that the larvae can munch their way through your precious collection is asking for trouble. Be sensible and keep your yarn wrapped up: in zip-lock bags, paper bags, boxes, whatever you have to hand. Storing your yarn in bags or boxes, preferably with some cedarwood or lavender sachets to hold the moths at bay, will keep your yarn protected and smelling fresh.

My Favourite Yarns

Choosing the right yarn for your project is everything and can make the difference between finishing the damn thing in a reasonable time and spying it months (or even years) later discarded and forgotten.

I am a yarn lover. In fact, like a lot of knitters, I am a yarn obsessive. I freakin' *love* the stuff. The yarns listed below are my favourites because they always motivate me to knit. You'll have your own favourites to obsess over soon enough but road-test some of these in the meantime – you won't be disappointed:

Malabrigo: possibly the most blogged-about yarn of all time, this super-soft pure merino-wool yarn comes from a little village in Uruguay and is available in a bewildering array of beautiful colours. My favourites are the kettle-dyed* worsted-weight (Aran) yarns and if I could only ever knit with one yarn for the rest of my knitting days, this would be it.

Koigi Premium Merino: a finely spun pure merino-wool 4-ply yarn. The yarn is hand-painted and I am in love with every single one of the hundred or so fabulous colours available, especially the almost neon-bright pinks, yellows and greens.

....

*All these different yarn-dying processes are a bit of minefield but here's a brief guide. In kettle-dying, the yarn is thrown in a pot with the dye once and once only. Unlike dip-dying, where the yarn is dipped into the pot several times to obtain the exact colour required, the results of kettle-dying are incredibly varied. Yarns can also be hand-painted, which means the yarn is laid flat and painted instead of being dipped in a pot. Then there's tie-dyed yarns, sprink-painted yarns and on and on …

Cascade 220: a very affordable pure wool Aran-weight yarn in a wide range of solid colours. Perfect for knitting huge things like blankets that take a lot of yarn. I have a stash of this yarn in about twenty colours that I'm planning on using to put together a huge granny square blanket as soon as I find the time.

Blue Sky Alpaca: I love the whole range of Blue Sky Alpaca's luxurious yarns, but the bulky-weight 50 per cent alpaca/50 per cent wool is my favourite. It's so unbelievably soft and smooth, perfect for fast but sumptuous knitting.

Manos Del Uruguay Handspun Semi-Solids: another fairtrade yarn from Uruguay, this chunky 100 per cent wool yarn isn't as soft as Malabrigo but the colours are heavenly.

Artesano 100% Alpaca: from the same company as Manos Del Uruguay, these super-soft yarns (which come in 4-ply, DK and Aran weight) are very reasonably priced and are available in some unusual, pretty colours.

Opal Sock Yarn: this self-patterning sock yarn comes in an astonishing range of colourways. I love knitting with self-patterning yarn; it's a thrill to see the intricate design magically appear on your needles.

Rowan Big Wool: a super-chunky pure merino-wool yarn that knits up fast as lightning. Perfect for last-minute scarves and cushions.

Shopping for Yarn

Whether you're buying yarn in your local yarn shop or online, you'll need to have a clear idea in your head about what it is you're looking for. If you're going to use the yarn suggested by your pattern, make sure you note the exact name of the yarn and the number of balls required. If you're being brave and using a substitute yarn, you'll also need to note down the yarn weight, needle size, tension and length of the yarn in the pattern. Having these details to hand when you are shopping will make the whole experience a lot easier.

Haberdasheries and Yarn Shops

I lived for years in a city with only a John Lewis to cater for my haberdashery needs; now yarn shops seem to be cropping up all over the place. For me, visiting a new yarn shop is the ultimate treat – I can while away hours feeling all the different yarns and dreaming up the perfect patterns to marry them with. I'm a total sucker for a super-soft yarn and often have to stop myself stroking them all against my face.

If you're new to knitting, visiting your local yarn shop with pattern in hand (or with the information you need written down) is the best way to get started – you get to cop a feel of the yarn you're after, can easily compare labels to find a substitute, pick the perfect colour, stock up on anything else you might need and, most importantly, you can ask for advice from yarn-obsessed staff who are usually more than happy to help you out. Chances are you'll have walked past your local yarn

If you're new to knitting, visiting your local yarn shop with pattern in hand (or with the information you need written down) is the best way to get started.

shop and stopped in front of the window to look at all the pretty things. But if you don't have a clue where your nearest shop is, or you're not lucky enough to live in a city that has woken up to the desperate need for a store, check out Knit Map (www.knitmap.com), a searchable catalogue of yarn shops around the world. As well as getting the address of your nearest shop, you can also read user-submitted reviews about what the shop stocks. (See 'Resources' for a list of my favourite yarn shops.)

Buying Online

Despite the fact that yarn shops are popping up all over the country, there are way more yarns ready and waiting to be tried than any shop could ever manage to stock.

I met a yarn over the internet once: his name was Malabrigo. Bloggers everywhere were going crazy for this super-soft Merino god from Uruguay. Seduced by pictures showing the truly beautiful kettle-dyed colours and tales of the yarn feeling like butter to knit, I desperately wanted to get my hands on some of this coveted string. Malabrigo is to be found everywhere these days but when I was looking for it a couple of years ago, none of my local yarn shops were stocking the stuff. So I searched on the web and found a tiny online shop in Wales that had some. The lovely lady who runs the store – her name is Lisa, and I'm still very grateful to her – even managed to get hold of the exact colour I was after (an especially scrumptious baby pink I had spotted on some blog or other). Lesson: when you're searching for the perfect yarn, the internet really is your best friend.

Buying yarn on the internet (and needles for that matter) needn't be a daunting task if you know exactly what you're looking for and can be a fun way of smoking out new yarns to try if you don't. As you won't have the yarn label in front of you, don't forget to pay careful attention to details about the yarn's composition (see p. 38). (See 'Resources' for a list of the best places to buy online.)

Lesson: when you're searching for the perfect yarn, the internet really is your best friend.

Secondhand

eBay (www.ebay.co.uk) is a great place to buy new or secondhand yarn if you know what you're after. It can be much cheaper than buying from a regular yarn shop, especially if you need a lot of the same yarn for a large project. It's also the place to search for discontinued yarns.

Charity shops often have baskets full of yarn on sale, but make sure you check for signs of a moth invasion before you buy (tiny white eggs buried within the fibres are an indication that the little bastards have set up their cosy home). Charity shops are also the place to pick up secondhand jumpers for unravelling and recycling.

How to Unravel a Charity Shop Jumper into a Ball of Yarn

Yeah, it sounds pretty miserly and more 'make do and mend' than chichi 'thrift', but it's actually quite fun to do and a great way to get your hands on a whole lot of expensive yarn for only a few pounds.

Choose a jumper that's made of thick yarn (thin yarn will break if you try to unravel it). No matter how fusty it might smell, don't be tempted to wash the jumper; you can carefully handwash the yarn once it's been unravelled.

Here's how you do it:

1 Turn the jumper inside out so that all the seams are clearly visible.

2 Using a seam ripper (or a pair of scissors), carefully rip (or snip) the little stitches that join the knitted pieces together. You might only need to snip one stitch before you're able to pull a thread that will unravel the full seam.

3 Repeat step 2 for each of the seams. You'll now have a pile of jumper bits.

4 Take one of the pieces and locate the cast-off edge. You should be able to spot a tail end of yarn that has been woven back into the fabric. If you pull this tail of yarn out from the edge, it will (hopefully) unravel the whole piece. If you can't easily find a yarn end, simply cut off the cast-off edge with a pair of scissors, grab a strand of yarn and start unravelling.

5 Repeat step 4 for every piece of the jumper, winding the yarn around a book as you go.

Soak the individual skeins (don't try doing it all at once – you'll get into a right tangle) in lukewarm water with a small amount of handwash detergent, then hang them up to dry over the bath. This will remove any foul pongs and relax the fibre if it's crimped.

Choosing Needles

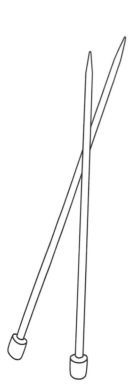

Now it's time to pick your pointers. Like yarn, needles come in all different shapes and sizes, from simple straights to fiddly circulars and mess-with-your-brain double-pointed ones. Here's what you need to know.

Material

In the olden days, needles was needles and all of them were made of steel. But we've come a long way since Mrs Montague was knitting those fancy French stockings for Queen Elizabeth and these days you can get your hands on needles made from a whole range of different materials. Needles have varying frictions and will grip the yarn differently depending on what they're made of.

Aluminium needles are the cheapest, the most widely available and up until fairly recently, they were the only kind you could get your hands on.* Because they are smooth and slippery, they're great for competent knitters who want (and are able) to knit super fast. They also make the most satisfying click when you're working away. But because they are so smooth, if you're not proficient with the pins, stitches have a tendency to slip off the end.

* In 1966, British spy George Blake escaped from Wormwood Scrubs (where he was serving a forty-two-year sentence for having been a double agent in the service of the KGB) using a nylon ladder with rungs reinforced with smuggled aluminium knitting needles. There's something James Bond-ish about this story, which makes perfect sense when you consider that before his MI6 days Blake worked in intelligence for the Royal Navy under Ian Fleming.

Plastic needles come in the prettiest of colours and are lightweight and flexible. I found a whole load of plastic needles at a car boot sale a few years ago and bought the lot for pennies. They look so good sitting in a tall glass vase but I rarely take them out for a ride because they just don't feel particularly nice in my hands. However, I know lots of knitters who are dedicated to their plastic pointers so the choice is yours.

Bamboo needles are the cashmere of needles. They are soft and smooth, and because they are rougher than aluminium needles, stitches are less likely to fall off the end, which makes them the perfect choice for beginners. Bamboo needles warm up as you knit, so they are flexible and easy on your hands. They are a little more expensive than metal needles and they can bend if you're knitting something heavy, like a very long and chunky scarf, so stick to using them for more lightweight projects.

Wooden needles are available in birch and exotic hardwoods like rosewood and ebony. They are pretty and strong but can be expensive.

The type of needles you choose to buy is entirely up to you but I strongly urge you go for bamboo (or wood if you can afford it). They make the whole experience of knitting so much more enjoyable and less stressful, they really are worth the extra cost. The Japanese company Clover make my favourite bamboo needles (as well as everything else you could possibly need to feed your knitting or crochet addiction) – check out their American website www.clover-usa.com and be amazed by the pleasing colours and cute Japanese packaging.

Bamboo needles are the cashmere of needles. They are soft and smooth, and because they are rougher than aluminium needles, stitches are less likely to fall off the end, which makes them the perfect choice for beginners.

Needle Size

Needles come in different sizes and lengths. The diameter of a needle is what determines its size and sizes range from 2mm to 25mm (although some old dear in Cornwall recently amused herself by breaking the Guinness world record for knitting on the world's largest needles – hers were 6.5cm in diameter and 3.5m long. Some knitters really do need to get out more). In the UK, needles are very sensibly named after their metric size; not so for the Americans – see the box on the next page for a handy conversion chart.

The size of your needle will determine the size of your knitting. Knitting with thick yarn on large needles will create a chunky, open fabric with big stitches while knitting with thin yarn on small needles will create a tighter-weave fabric with little stitches.

When it comes to straight knitting needles, length isn't the most important thing in the world. If you're knitting something particularly wide that calls for you to cast on a large number of stitches, you'll want to use some nice long needles so that all your stitches fit on the needle without too much bunching up, but you can knit little things on any length of needles. Length becomes more significant when you're dealing with circulars (see below).

UK/US Needle Conversion Chart

In the UK, we cleverly name our needles after their metric size. But this hasn't always been the case and if you get your hand on a pair of Grandma's needles, they are likely to have a number printed on the stopper that doesn't relate to the metric size. And just to confuse things further, the Americans use a different system altogether.

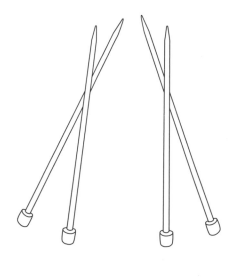

Metric	Old UK	US
2mm	14	0
2.25mm	13	1
2.75mm	12	2
3mm	11	–
3.25mm	10	3
3.5mm	–	4
3.75mm	9	5
4mm	8	6
4.5mm	7	7
5mm	6	8
5.5mm	5	9
6mm	4	10
6.5mm	3	10.5
7mm	2	–
7.5mm	1	–
8mm	0	11
9mm	00	13
10mm	000	15
12mm	–	17
16mm	–	19
19mm	–	35
25mm	–	50

Circular and Double-Pointed Needles

When most people think of knitting needles, they think of the simple straight kind with a stopper on one end and a point at the other. But there's more to the needle game than this. If you want to knit a tube structure with no seams, you'll need to knit in the round (which means you knit continuously, i.e., not in rows but in a spiral) using either circular needles or double-pointed needles. Hats, socks and wristwarmers are all things that are knitted in the round.

Circular needles are ugly-looking things, two short needles connected with a flexible plastic wire. Like straight needles, circulars come in different sizes but they also come in lots of different lengths. Length is essential when you're knitting on circulars in the round because the length of your needles determines the circumference of your tube – while you can knit a *larger* tube on shorter circular needles, it is impossible to knit a tube *smaller* than the length of your circular needles.

Circular needles can also be used to knit in the same way you do on straights (by simply not joining your knitting in the round) and because circular needles are available in very long lengths, they can be useful when you're knitting something particularly wide, like a blanket.

Double-pointed needles (DPNs) are like your regular straight needles but instead of having a stopper on one end, they have two pointed ends. That's rather obvious. DPNs come in packs of four or five and are used all at once to knit in the round. Although they are a bit more of a hassle to negotiate, the advantage of DPNs over circulars is that the length of your DPNs doesn't have to determine the circumference of your tube.

Shopping for Needles

You can pick up new knitting needles, straight, circular or double-pointed, anywhere you can buy your yarn. The fancier yarns shops will stock a lovely range of bamboo and wooden needles as well as boring aluminium ones. However, I buy pretty much all of my needles on eBay – brand-new pairs of Clover bamboo needles are a fraction of the cost of the ones in the shops.

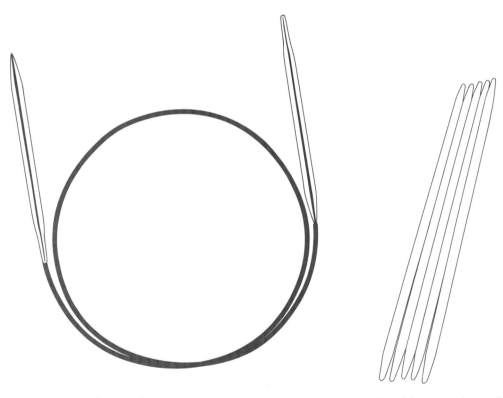

Circular needles   Double-pointed needles / DPNs

Knitting Tools

While one of the great joys of knitting is the fact that you don't need lots of expensive tools and equipment to get started – really, yarn and needles are the only absolute essentials – once you get beyond knitting simple scarves, there are a few extras you will want to invest in. Get yourself a pretty little make-up bag to house your kit and keep everything to hand while you're knitting.

Scissors: for snipping your yarn when you're ready to cast off and trimming yarn ends that are to be woven back into your fabric. Any kind of scissors will do but I like little embroidery ones that fit inside my tool bag.

Tapestry needles: also referred to as yarn needles or finishing needles, these are just larger versions of regular sewing needles with blunt ends. You'll need one to sew in your yarn ends, for seaming (see pp. 88–93) and for working duplicate stitch (see p. 84).

Pins: for pinning your knitted pieces to the carpet/bed/dog when you're blocking (see p. 94) and for keeping your knitted pieces in place when you're sewing up seams.

Tape measure: for measuring knitted pieces. Lots of patterns will tell you to knit until your piece is a certain length instead of counting out the number of rows you need to knit. A tape measure is also vital for measuring your tension square (see pp. 100–101).

Row counter: for keeping track of the number of rows you have knitted. Very useful when you're working lots of rows in the same stitch and need to keep count without losing your mind (or really pissing off the person sitting next to you on the sofa/train/in the pub). Row counters usually have a hole in the middle for you to stick your needle through so you know to notch it up when you get to the end of a row, but I prefer the 'clicker' type, like the one shown here, just because that click is so freakin' satisfying (and you got to get your clicks where you can).

Stitch markers: there are two kinds of stitch markers shown here. The first is a ring marker: slip this little guy on to your needle between stitches to mark your place in a row or to remind you where you need to do something special, like increase or decrease. They are particularly useful to mark the beginning of a row when you're knitting in the round and it isn't so obvious where the circle begins and ends. When you reach your ring marker, you simply transfer it from your left-hand needle to your right and carry on knitting. The other kind shown here is a split-ring marker; these can be used in the same ways as ring markers but they can also, very handily, be 'clipped' on to your work (attached to a stitch) at any time.

Stitch holders: for holding stitches that need to be kept aside to be worked on later. Huge safety pins would also do the job. Or if you're being really thrifty, you can slip the stitches on to a scrap piece of yarn instead (although getting those stitches back on to the needle can be fiddly).

Cable needles: these funny-looking pins are used to make cables (see p. 85). You put stitches on hold while you knit the next lot of stitches on the needle and then go back and knit the stitches off the cable needle. Cable needles can be straight, bendy in the middle or U-shaped; which shape you use is down to personal preference. If you don't have a cable needle to hand, a small double-pointed needle will work just as well.

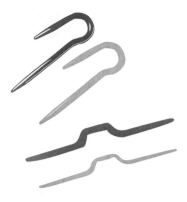

Crochet hook: to pick up the dreaded dropped stitch (see pp. 96–7). You only really need one crochet hook in a small size, so root around in your grandma's sewing box – you'll be sure to find one somewhere.

Point protectors: more useful to stop your work falling off the ends of your needles when storing mid-project (particularly when you're knitting with circulars) than to protect your points but they will stop the tips of your precious bamboo and wooden needles becoming rough and damaged.

Needle gauge: because not all needles have a handy inscription about size, this tool is useful to measure the diameter of your knitting needles so you know what size they are. Just keep prodding until you find a hole that fits.

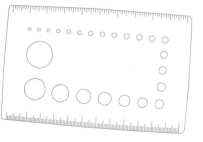

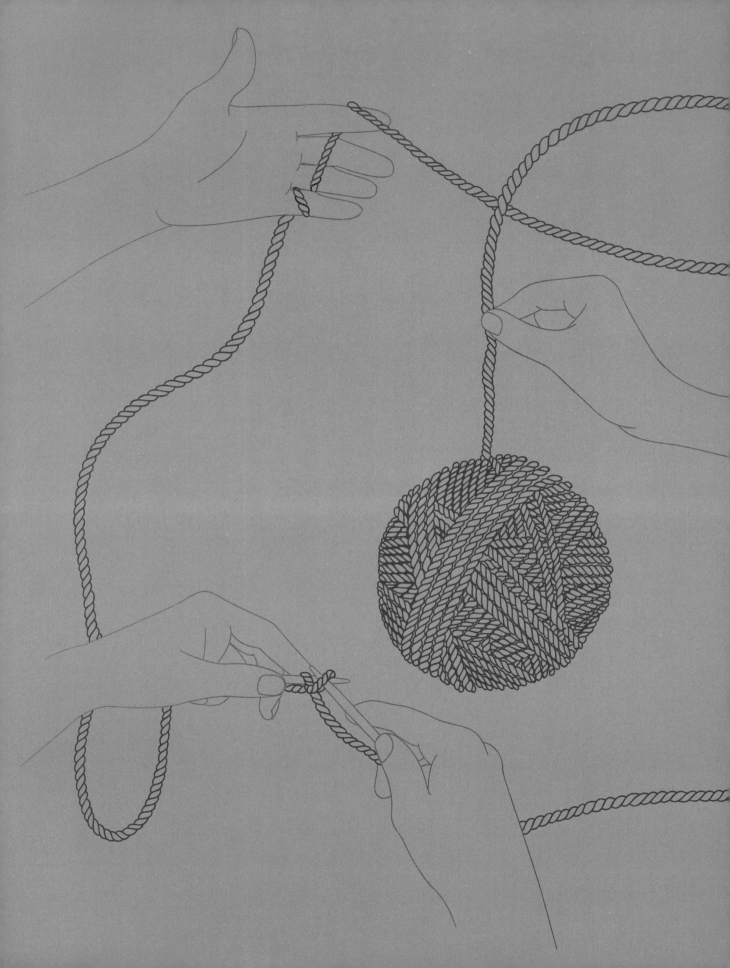

I spent a lot of time in a funked-up state of frustration when I was teaching myself to knit. All the terms and instructions were so foreign to me I'd rarely understand them first time. I did a lot of swearing.

But then, most of the time, once I had read the instructions a few times over, slowly and carefully (and often, rather embarrassingly, out loud), something would eventually click and I'd hungrily move on to the next step. So pay heed to this little pep talk: yes, you will feel like you're being asked to learn the language of an alien species, and yes, it will be frustrating. But you will get it eventually and it will be worth it. So take a deep breath, make yourself a cup of hippy tea and persevere.

Don't go reading this whole section at once - we're about to cover a lot of ground and there's a good chance you'll frighten yourself right back to your cross stitch. Learn how to cast on, make a knit stitch and a purl stitch and how to cast off, and then get practising with your first scarf. Come back to the more complicated instructions as and when you need them.

Now, let's get on with it ...

Casting On

Getting your first lot of stitches on to your needles is called casting on and this is where it all begins. There are lots of different ways to cast on. Some methods will give you a strong, firm edge while others will give you a softer, more elastic edge. I am going to show you three ways of casting on because once you get a bit more proficient, it's useful to be able to choose the method that will give you the perfect cast-on edge for your pattern. I would suggest you either start by learning the knitting-on method and ignore the other two until you feel ready or try having a go at all three methods and then stick to the one that works best for you.

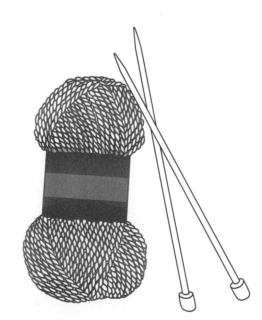

How to Make a Slip Knot

Whichever method to cast on you choose, you'll need to begin by making a slip knot. This will become your first cast-on stitch.

1

Unwind a strand of yarn about 10cm long and hold it in your left hand between your thumb and forefinger with the ball of yarn sitting to your right. Take hold of the yarn further up towards the ball with your right hand and wrap it clockwise around your left forefinger and middle fingers so that you make a loop.

2

Using your right hand, grab the yarn attached to the ball and pull a new loop through the loop on your fingers.

3

Keep pulling the loop in your right hand until the loop on your left hand drops off your fingers. This is your slip knot.

4

Slide your slip knot on to one of your knitting needles and tighten by pulling on both yarn ends. There you have your first cast-on stitch!

Now to get the rest of your stitches on the needle …

Knitting On

This method calls for two needles and a bit of patience. It will create a nice loose edge, perfect for the more rigid stitch patterns, like stocking stitch.

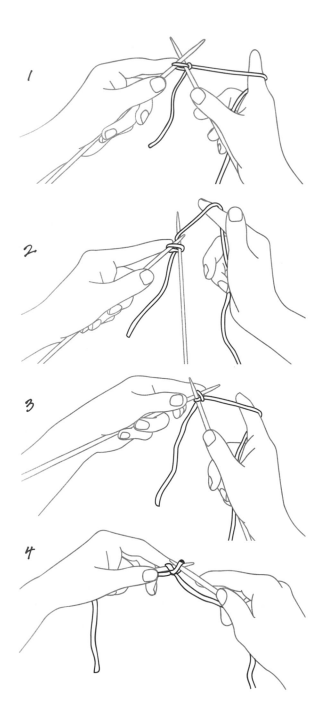

1

With your skip knot on your left needle, slide the point of your right needle into the front of the loop so that your needles make a cross with the right needle under the left.

2

Now pay attention: grab the yarn end that's attached to the ball and wrap it around the tip of your right needle in an anticlockwise direction.

3

Using your right forefinger to hold the yarn taut, pivot the point of your right needle under and in front of your left needle so that you grab the little loop you just made on your right needle. At this point, your right needle should be in front of the left.

4

Allow the new loop to loosen up by pulling the right needle away from the left, then transfer it to your left needle by sliding the point of your left needle into the middle of the loop and letting it drop off the right needle.

Now you have two stitches! Repeat steps 1 to 4, making loops and adding them to your left needle until you have the desired number of cast-on stitches.

Cable Cast-On

Very similar to the knitting-on method shown above, the cable cast-on creates a sturdier edge. It's more fiddly than knitting-on but the results are more solid and more attractive.

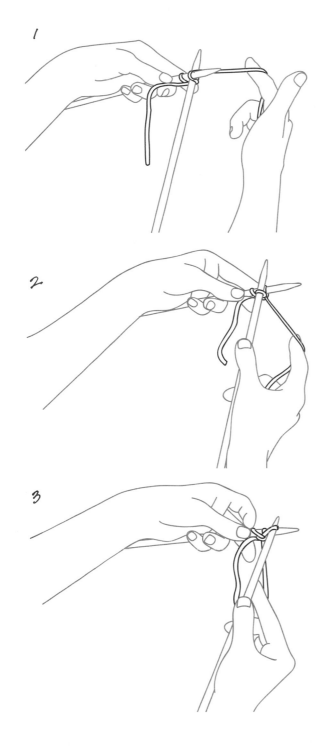

1

Make a slip knot and cast on another stitch using the knitting-on method shown above. You now have two stitches on your needle. Insert the point of your right needle *between* the first two stitches on the left needle and wrap the yarn around the right needle in an anticlockwise direction.

2

Bring the new loop to the front by pivoting the point of your right needle under and in front of your left needle.

3

Transfer the stitch on to the left needle by sliding the point of your left needle into the middle of the loop and letting it drop off the right needle.

Now you have three stitches. Repeat the steps, making loops between stitches and adding them to your left needle until you have the desired number of cast-on stitches.

Thumb Method

Using just one needle and your fingers and thumb, this method is super fast but takes a little while to get your head around. It creates a nice elastic edge to your work, the perfect partner to more stretchy stitches like garter stitch or rib stitch and for projects that will be stretched like hats or wristwarmers. For this method, you'll be making stitches using the tail end of the yarn so when you are making your slip knot, you'll need to leave a tail at least three times the width of the piece you want to knit.

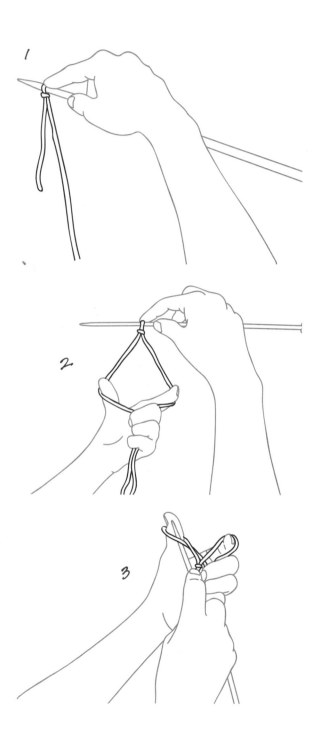

1

Hold the needle in your right hand and position the yarn so that the tail is on the left and the ball end on the right. Place your right forefinger on top of the slip knot to hold it in place.

2

Insert your left thumb and forefinger through the two strands of yarn from back to front and grab the yarn ends with the bottom three fingers of your left hand, then stretch out your thumb and forefinger to make a sort of catapult shape.

3

Pick up the strand of yarn from the front of your thumb with the point of your right needle.

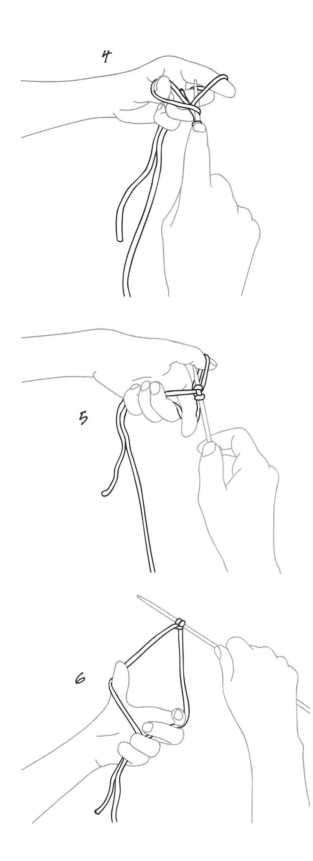

4

Now here's the tricky bit: wrap the yarn on your left forefinger around the needle in an anticlockwise direction.

5

Lift the loop of yarn on your left thumb over the tip of the needle and let it drop off your thumb.

6

Pull the tail end of the yarn to tighten the stitch. Now you have two stitches . . .

. . . and probably a bit of a sore head. This method of casting on is difficult to get the hang of at first – it can feel like an unnecessarily fiddly game of cat's cradle – but once you get it, it's efficient and looks very impressive to the passer-by.

Holding Your Yarn and Needles

Now then, before we can get down to the actual knitting (and that's to come really soon, I promise), you should learn how to actually hold your sticks and string. Being a beginner is not an excuse to develop bad habits and if you can learn to hold your yarn and needles in the correct way from day one, I can guarantee you'll find this whole knitting game easier (and faster) in the long run.

Here's how I like to hold my yarn:

With your right hand, wrap the yarn anticlockwise around your little finger, over your two middle fingers and then around your forefinger. Like this:

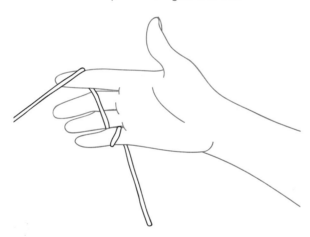

Now gently close your bottom three fingers around the yarn to stop it jumping out of your hand. Make sure you don't hold the yarn too tightly or it won't feed smoothly from ball to needle.

Here's how I hold my needles:

Pick up the needle with the stitches on with your left hand and loosely grasp it with your thumb and forefinger resting just behind the first stitch on the needle. With your yarn held using the method shown above, pick up the other needle with your right hand, rest your thumb about 10cm from the point of the needle and point your forefinger straight in front of you. Like this:

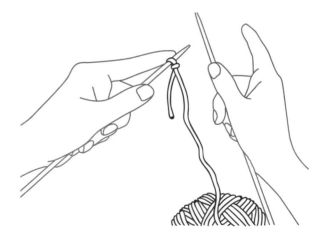

The Stitches

Now you know how to cast on and hold your needles and yarn in the correct way, it's time to get down to the knitty-gritty and learn how to knit and purl.

There are two ways to make knit and purl stitches: English and Continental. Their names don't really mean a great deal these days – I have seen knitters from all over the world using both methods. The English method, holding the working yarn in the right hand, is older* and more popular than the Continental style (originating from Germany, according to knit historian Richard Rutt), which has you holding the yarn in the left hand – perhaps because it's easier to get the hang of. (Although if you know what you're doing, the Continental method is much faster. Elizabeth Zimmermann used to swear by it and I've come to find that she was right about most things.) Anyway, I'm going to teach you how to knit using the English method exclusively, because this is the method I use, it's the method my mother and grandmother use and the method most of the knitters I know use.

....

* Those paintings of the knitting Madonna from fourteenth-century Europe show her holding the yarn in her right hand.

How to Make a Knit Stitch

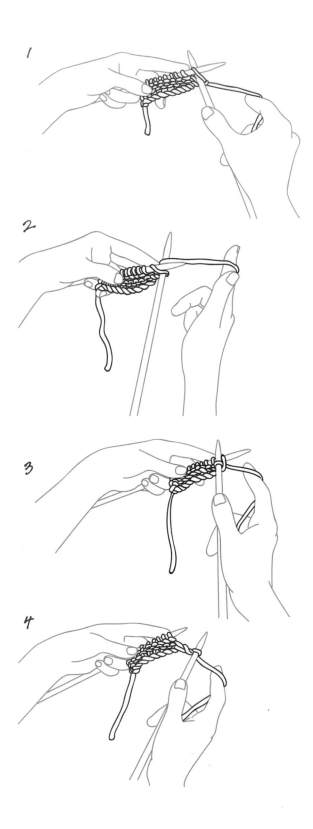

1

2

3

4

When making knit stitches, the yarn is always held at the *back* of the work and the right needle is inserted through the loops on the left needle from *front* to *back*.

1

With the yarn at the back of your work, insert the point of your right needle into the first stitch on your left needle from front to back so that your needles make a cross with the right under the left.

2

Wrap the yarn around the point of your right needle in an anticlockwise direction.

3

Using your right forefinger to hold the yarn taut, pivot the point of your right needle under and in front of your left needle so that you grab the little loop you just made on your right needle. At this stage, your right needle should be in front of the left.

4

Now slide your right needle to the right until the loop on the left needle drops off the end. Congratulations – you have just made your first knit stitch!

Repeat steps 1 to 4, knitting the stitches on the left needle until there are no more left to knit. When you are done, you will have transferred all the stitches to your right needle and your left will be empty. Now simply switch hands, turning your work around as you go, so that the needle full of newly knitted stitches is in your left hand and the right needle is free to knit them again. Keep going like this, knitting a row, switching hands and knitting back again and that's it – you're knitting!

How to Make a Purl Stitch

A purl stitch is basically a knit stitch in reverse. When making purl stitches, the yarn is always held at the *front* of the work and the right needle is inserted through the loops on the left needle from *back* to *front*.

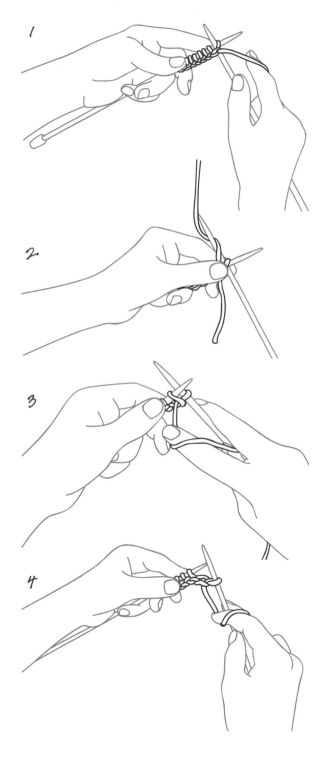

1

With your yarn in front of your work this time, insert the point of your right needle into the first stitch on the left needle from back to front so that your needles make a cross with the right needle in front of the left.

2

Wrap the yarn around the point of your right needle in an anticlockwise direction.

3

Carefully slide your right needle down until you can pivot the point down and under the left needle so that the loop you have just made by wrapping the yarn around the needle is sitting on your right needle.

4

Let the loop on the left needle slip off and say hello to your first purl stitch!

Stitch Patterns

The knit stitch and the purl stitch are the only two stitches there are in knitting. Seriously, all those fancy-pants stitch patterns I'm sure you're dying to try are really only combinations and variations of these two basic stitches. The most common stitch patterns are garter stitch, stocking stitch, rib stitch and moss stitch.

Garter Stitch

All rows: K

Garter stitch is the most basic stitch of the lot and is produced by simply knitting every row. Because a purl stitch is a back-to-front knit stitch, if you purl every row, you'll also get garter stitch. But purling stitches is trickier than knitting them (as I'm sure you've realized by now) and I don't know anyone who uses all purl to make garter stitch – that would be foolish. Garter stitch is strong, firm and reversible. It also lies flat so it's great for making scarves.

* You'll come across patterns referring to the right side (abbreviated as RS) and the wrong side (WS) all the time. It's fairly self-explanatory: the right side refers to the side of your work that will end up facing out and the wrong side will be the side facing in.

Stocking Stitch

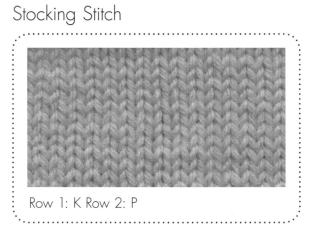

Row 1: K Row 2: P

Stocking stitch is the most popular stitch of the lot and is produced by alternating rows of knits and purls: i.e., you knit every stitch on row one, purl every stitch on row two, knit every stitch on row three and so on. Because a purl stitch is simply the reverse of a knit stitch, alternating them in this way will give you a fabric with all the tidy little 'v's on one side (the right side) and all the funny little bumps on the other (the wrong side).* Stocking stitch is smooth and stretchy but because it isn't reversible, it will curl in at the edges, so it's usually used to make tubular things and needs a reversible stitch border (like garter stitch) to make flat things. Above is the right side, looking all professional and pretty.

Rib Stitch

All rows: K2, p2

Rib stitch patterns are produced by lining up the 'v's and bumps vertically in columns. To make rib stitch, you alternate knit and purl stitches within a row and then knit the knits and purl the purls on the following rows. It produces a more elastic fabric than stocking stitch and because it's reversible, it lies nice and flat. You can make your columns of 'v's and bumps as wide as you like but the one you'll most commonly be required to use is a 2x2 rib. Here's how you do it:

Cast on a multiple of 4 stitches. (You'll hear this direction to cast on a multiple of a certain number of stitches a lot; it basically means that you need to make sure that your total number of cast-on stitches is divisible by that number. In this case it's 4 – so you would cast on 16 stitches or 20 stitches or 24 stitches and so on.)

Row 1: knit the first two stitches. Now bring the yarn round to the front and purl two stitches. Take the yarn round to the back and knit two stitches. Keep alternating between two knit stitches and two purl stitches until you get to the end of the row. You should end with two purl stitches.

Row 2: do exactly the same as you did with row 1 – knit two stitches, purl two stitches and alternate like this until you get to the end of the row.

And that's it: keep repeating rows 1 and 2 until you have a nice long length of ribbed fabric.

Moss Stitch

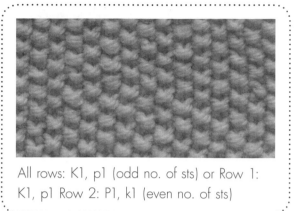

All rows: K1, p1 (odd no. of sts) or Row 1: K1, p1 Row 2: P1, k1 (even no. of sts)

Moss stitch is by far my favourite stitch – there's something about those tidy little bumps that makes me come over all nostalgic for baby blankets and Laura Ashley cardigans. Sometimes called seed stitch,* moss stitch is strong, reversible and won't go curly on your ass. Moss stitch is made by alternating knits and purls on every stitch. To make moss stitch, cast on an uneven number of stitches and for every row, knit one, purl one, knit one and so on until you reach the end of the row. You should always start and finish with a knit stitch. To make moss stitch with an even number of cast-on stitches, start with a knit stitch on row one and a purl stitch on row two.

That's enough stitch patterns for now. See pp. 105–109 for a load more variations to try.

....

* There is a school of thought that says moss stitch and seed stitch are different things but the names are widely used interchangeably.

Casting Off

When you've finished working your rows of garter stitch, stocking stitch, rib stitch or moss stitch, you'll need to cast your work off your needles in such a way that it doesn't just unravel in your lap. This is called casting off (or binding off if you're in America). Casting off is simple and satisfying.

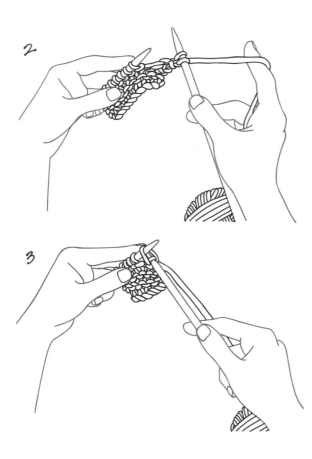

1

Knit the first stitch on your left needle in the normal way.

2

Knit the next stitch on your left needle in the normal way. You now have two stitches on your right needle.

3

With the point of your left needle, pick up the first stitch on your right needle, lift it up and over the second stitch and let it drop off the point of the right needle.

Casting Off in Pattern

You've just learned how to cast off using knit stitches but there will be times when you'll want to cast off using purl stitches so that your cast-off edge matches the pattern of your fabric. It really isn't complicated – for steps 1 and 2, simply purl your stitches instead of knitting them.

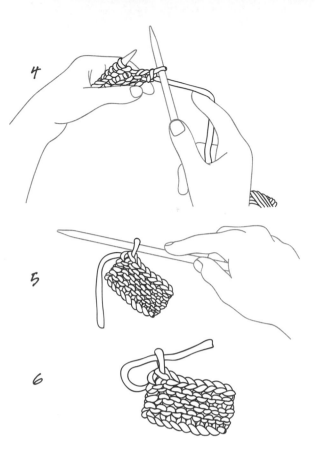

4

You now have one stitch remaining on the right needle.

5

Repeat steps 2 to 3, knitting a stitch, then lifting the first stitch over the second and off the needle, until you have one remaining stitch on your right needle. Cut the end of the yarn leaving a short tail of 10–15cm.

6

Carefully slip the last stitch off your left needle without letting the loop unravel, thread the end of yarn through the loop and pull it tight.

How to start a new ball of yarn and weave in yarn ends

When you're knitting something long like a scarf, you'll usually need to use more than one ball of yarn. It's best to start a new ball of yarn at the beginning of a row so that you don't end up with any big ugly lumps in the middle of your nice neat work. Here's what you do:

1 Unravel a good 10–15cm of your new yarn and grab hold of the tail along with the tail end of your old yarn with your left hand. (These tail ends are called 'yarn ends'; when a pattern tells you to weave in your yarn ends, these little leftover tails are what it is referring to).

2 Start knitting using the new yarn. The first stitch you knit will feel a little strange and loose but keep going until you get to the end of the row.

3 Go back and loosely tie together the two yarn ends left at the other end of the row so that your work doesn't start to unravel.

4 Once you've cast off your work, go back and untie all the little knots you made, then use a tapestry needle (a bigger, blunter version of a regular sewing needle) to weave those loose yarn ends back into your work – you can do this either vertically up the side of your work or horizontally at the back of your work by weaving in and out of the bumps without going through to the front.

Practice Makes Perfect

Right, it's time to stop studying and start putting your new skills into practice, because you now know enough to make your first scarf. Exciting!

Pick your stitch pattern – it's probably best to start with garter stitch because it's so simple but if you're feeling daring, have a go with moss stitch or a rib stitch (just don't try stocking stitch; the edges will curl in and leave you with an odd looking tubular thing). Invest in some nice big needles and some chunky yarn and then all you have to do is this:

1 Cast on.

2 Knit in your chosen stitch pattern until your scarf is the desired length.

3 Cast off.

That's it! It couldn't be easier, right?

How to make stripes

Now you know how to start a new ball of yarn, you can also experiment with making stripes. Big fat stripes are easy to make – just follow the steps on the previous page for starting a new ball of yarn, changing colours as you go.

If little stripes are more your thing, you can get away with keeping two balls of yarn (or more if you're really brave) going at the same time. When you get to the end of a row and are ready to change colour, pick up your new colour yarn and

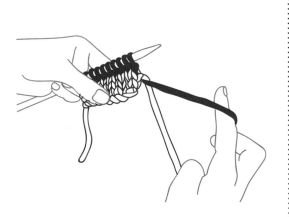

let the old colour hang there ready to pick up once you want to change colour again. When you are ready to switch, simply twist the two yarn ends together before you knit the first stitch on a row.

Shaping

Once you're ready to move beyond knitting rectangles and squares, you'll need to know how to make your knitting wider or narrower by increasing or decreasing the number of stitches on your needles. This is called shaping.

Increasing

There are a few different ways to increase the number of stitches on your needles and your pattern will usually let you know which method to use.

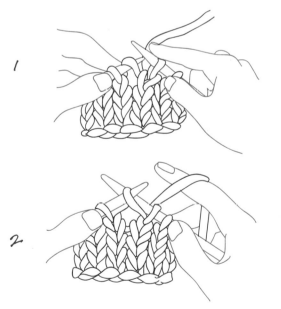

Make One (m1)

The make-one increase creates a new stitch between two existing stitches and has the benefit of being pretty much invisible. Knit to the point where your pattern calls for you to make one (m1), then:

1 With the point of your left needle, pick up the strand of yarn that sits between the stitch you just knitted and the next stitch on the needle from front to back.

2 Now here's the wonky bit: insert the point of your right needle into the *back* of this new stitch (it feels weird, I know) and knit it just as if it were a normal stitch.

It's really important that you remember to knit into the *back* of the stitch in step 2, otherwise you'll create a big hole below it.

Working a m1 on a purl row: to make one between two purl stitches, purl into the back of the picked-up stitch instead of knitting into it.

Increase One (inc1)

This method makes two stitches out of one by knitting into the front *and* the back of the same stitch. It is more visible than the make-one increase method because it leaves a little horizontal bar across the bottom of the new stitch. Knit to the point where your pattern calls for you to increase one (inc1), then:

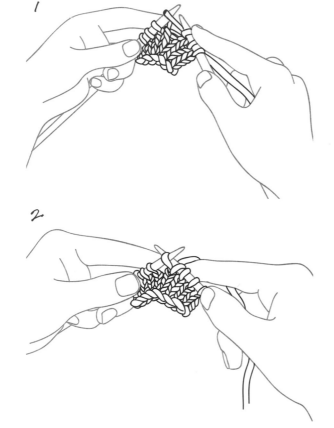

1

Knit the next stitch as usual but don't let it drop of the left needle.

2

Now knit into the back of that same stitch and let it drop off the needle.

Sometimes a pattern will call for you to knit into the front and back of a stitch (the abbreviation is 'KFB'), and this is the method you use.

Working an inc1 on a purl row: to increase one between two purl stitches, purl into the front and back of the stitch instead of knitting into it.

Yarn Over (yo)

The easiest method of them all, a yarn-over increase creates a new stitch by simply wrapping the yarn around your needle between stitches. Making a stitch in this way will create a big hole in your work, but that's okay because some patterns want you to make such a hole. Knit to the point where your pattern calls for you to make a yarn over (yo), then:

1

Bring your yarn to the front of your work, just as you would if you were about to make a purl stitch.

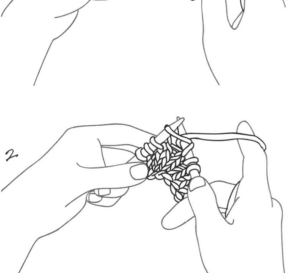

2

With your yarn in front, knit the next stitch.

You'll see that by bringing your yarn to front of your work before knitting the next stitch, you have created an extra loop on your right needle. This is your newly created stitch.

Working a yo on a purl row: to make a yarn over between two purl stitches, take your yarn to the back of your work and then back to the front by wrapping it anticlockwise around the right needle, then purl the next stitch as normal.

Increasing by Casting On

If you want to make your work wider by a number of stitches at the beginning or end of a row, you'll need to cast more stitches on to the needle. You can do this using the cable cast-on method:

1

Insert the point of your right needle *between* the first two stitches on the left needle, wrap the yarn around the needle and bring the new loop to the front between these two stitches.

2

Transfer the stitch on to the left needle by sliding the point of your left needle into the middle of the loop and letting it drop off the right needle.

Repeat steps 1 and 2 until you have cast on the desired number of stitches. You'll now be able to knit across in the usual way.

To cast on stitches in the middle of a row:

Knit to the point where you are required to cast on stitches, then:

1

Turn your work around so that the stitches you have just knitted are on the left needle (you are essentially flipping the work over so that the wrong side is now facing you). Your yarn will be at the front at this point so take it around to the back.

2

Follow steps 1 and 2 above until you have cast on the required number of stitches.

3

Turn your work around again, take the yarn to the back and continue knitting.

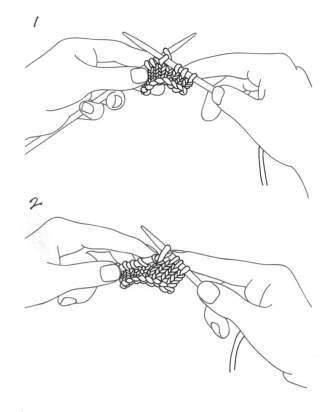

Decreasing

Decreasing stitches will make a little angle in your work, slanting either to the right or the left – something you don't have to worry about when you're increasing. The first method described below (k2tog) creates a right-slanting decrease, the last two (ssk and skp) create a left-slanting decrease.

Knit Two Together (k2tog)

Easy-peasy, this one – you just knit two stitches together at the same time. Use this method to create a right-slanting decrease. Knit to the point where your pattern calls for you to knit two together (k2tog), then:

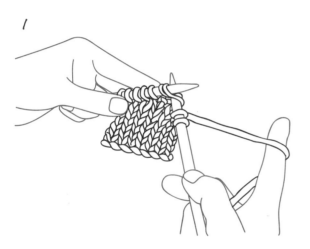

1

Slide the point of your right needle into the next *two* stitches on your left needle.

2

Wrap your yarn around and knit these two stitches together (just as you would if they were one) and let both stitches drop off the left needle.

You can also knit three together (k3tog) in exactly the same way: slide the point of your right needle into the next three stitches and knit them together as above.

Working a k2tog on a purl row: exactly the same as above, except you purl two stitches together instead of knitting them.

Slip, Slip, Knit (ssk)

Another way to knit two stitches together but this time, you'll create a left-slanting decrease. Knit to the point where your pattern calls for you to slip, slip, knit (ssk), then:

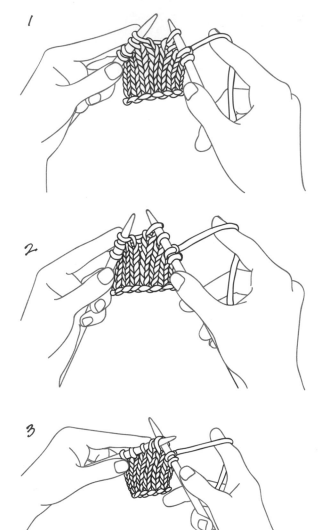

1

Slide the point of your right needle into the next stitch but instead of wrapping the yarn around and knitting it, just left it slip off your left needle.

2

Slip the next stitch exactly as you did above.

3

Slide the point of your left needle into the front of the two slipped stitches.

4

Knit these two stitches together (just as you would if they were one) and let them drop off the left needle.

A Note on Slipping Stitches

Slipping stitches from your left needle to your right as if to knit is called slipping knitwise. Sometimes you'll need to slip stitches purlwise – all you need to do is slide the needle into the next stitch as if you were going to purl and slip it on to your right needle. When you are slipping stitches to decrease, you should always slip knitwise. Often, your pattern will tell you to slip a stitch (the abbreviation is 'sl') not because you need to decrease but just because you need to slip a stitch (you'll see this in lots of lace stitch patterns); in these cases you should always slip that stitch purlwise.

Slip, Knit, Pass Slipped Stitch over (skp)

Another decrease that slants to the left, this method is a bit fiddly but you'll get the hang of it after a few goes. Knit to the point where your pattern calls for you to slip, knit and pass the slipped stitch over (skp), then:

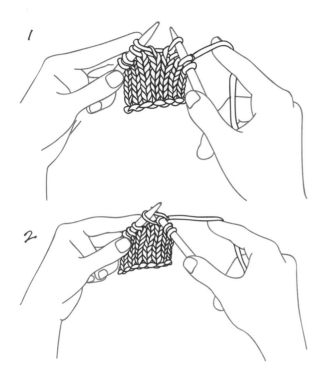

1
Slide the point of your right needle into the next stitch but instead of wrapping the yarn around and knitting it, just left it slip off your left needle (i.e., slip the stitch knitwise).

2
Knit the next stitch as normal.

3
Now here's the fiddly bit: with the point of your left needle, pick up and lift the slipped stitch up and over the knitted stitch and let it drop off the right needle.

Decreasing by Casting Off

Just as you can increase by casting on, so you can decrease by casting off. Usually you cast off stitches at the beginning of a row but casting off in the middle of a row uses just the same method:

1
Knit the first two stitches, then pass the first stitch over the second, as you would normally do when casting off.

2
Knit the next stitch and pass the first stitch over the second.

3
Repeat step 2 until you have cast off the required number of stitches.

4
Carry on knitting across your row.

Picking Up Stitches

Sometimes you'll need to pick up the stitches along a seam so that you can start knitting on them as if they were a cast-on edge. You'll need to do this if you want to add a border to your work or if you want to turn a heel on a pair of socks, for example.

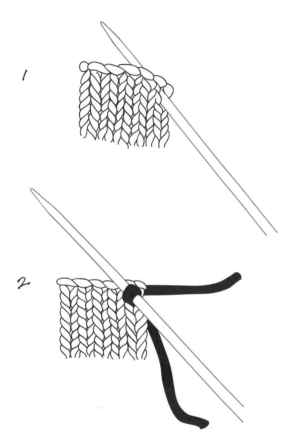

Picking up stitches along a cast-off edge:

1
Holding the work in your left hand with the cast-off edge at the top, insert the point of your right needle into the first full stitch beneath the cast-off row.

2
Wrap the yarn around the needle as if you were going to knit and pull the loop back through to the front of your work. You've just picked up a stitch.

3
Now insert your right needle (with the picked-up stitch on it) into the next stitch along the row, wrap the yarn around the needle and pull the loop through as you did in step 2. Keep going like this until you've picked up the required number of stitches.

Picking up stitches along a selvedge (side edge):

Usually when your pattern calls for you to pick up stitches along a side edge, you will have already created a tidy chain-edge seam along the sides (made by slipping the first stitch of every row; see p. 94 for more on edge stitches), which makes it much easier to pick up stitches.

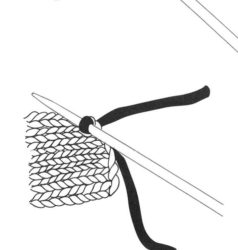

1

Holding your work in your left hand with the side edge on top, insert the point of your right needle underneath the first 'v' of the chain edge.

2

Wrap your yarn around the needle as if you were going to knit and pull the loop back through to the front of your work. You've just picked up a stitch.

3

Now insert your right needle (with the picked-up stitch on it) underneath the next 'v' and do the same. Keep going like this, picking up as many stitches as your pattern tells you to.

Knitting in the Round

Knitting 'in the round' allows you to create tubes of fabric without any nasty-looking seams on display (although seams need not be nasty looking – see pp. 88–93). To knit in the round, you need either a pair of circular needles (I don't really know why they are called a pair when you can't get singular circulars) or a set of double-pointed needles.

Knitting in the round only looks difficult but, really, it isn't hard.

Lots of people find the idea of knitting in the round terrifying – it looks all fiddly and difficult and just so different from the straight kind of knitting we are all used to. In fact, I know some really quite experienced knitters who actively avoid projects that involve knitting in the round because they just don't think they'll be able to handle it. These poor quivering souls are missing out on knitting some really fun things – socks, hats and gloves are all things that are knitted in the round. Please, please, please take this on board: knitting in the round only *looks* difficult but, really, it isn't hard. Plus, and this *is* a bonus, because the right side of your work is always facing you, knitting in the round means you can knit stocking stitch without ever having to make a purl stitch, which is a real boon for those of us who hate to purl.

Using Circular Needles

The length of your circular needles will determine the circumference of your knitted tube – remember, you can't knit a tube smaller than the length of your circular needles so make sure your needles are smaller than the required circumference of your tube.* Your pattern should tell you what needle length is required.

To knit in the round using circular needles:

1

Cast on the required number of stitches. Then bring the tips of your needles together to create a circle with your first cast-on stitch on your left and your last cast-on stitch (with the ball of yarn attached) on your right.

2

Make sure that all your stitches are pointing in the same direction and none are twisted. Then slide the point of your right needle into the front of the first stitch on the left needle and start knitting.

And that's all there is to it – see, it's not so complicated, is it?

Because you're technically knitting in a spiral, when you're knitting on circular needles, it isn't easy to see where a row begins and ends. You can mark the beginning of the row by slipping a stitch marker on to your needle between the last stitch of one row and the first stitch of the next. (When you reach the marker, just transfer it from your left needle to your right and carry on knitting.)

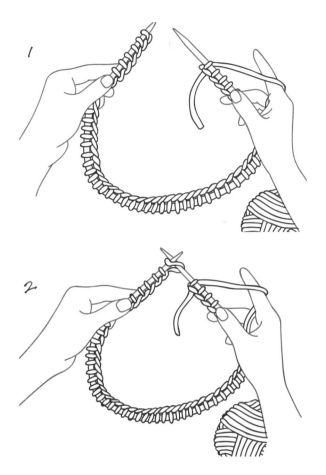

1

2

* I told a little lie there. There is actually a way to knit smaller tubes on larger circular needles, by using a really long circular and a technique called magic-loop knitting. If you can't get your head around using double-pointed needles, it might be worth giving this way of knitting in the round a whirl. I have never had a problem using DPNs so I don't bother with magic-loop knitting, but I know lots of knitters who swear by it. It's a little complicated to explain in words so if you fancy having a go, just type 'magic-loop knitting' into Google and you'll find an instructional video to show you what it's all about.

Using Double-Pointed Needles

Knitting with double-pointed needles looks like a pretty impressive feat of manual dexterity but, again, it really isn't as complex as it looks. The advantage of using double-pointed needles over circulars is that you don't have to have a particular length of needles – you can knit tiny tubes on any length of double-pointed needles. DPNs come in packs of five but usually you'll just use four: three needles to hold the stitches and one to knit them with.

To knit in the round using double-pointed needles:

1

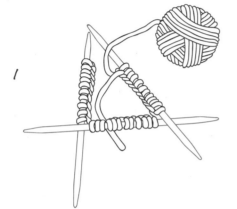

Cast on the required number of stitches on to one double-pointed needle. Slip the first third of these stitches on to a second double-pointed needle and slip the last third on to a third needle (the middle third will stay on the original needle). Then bend the three needles into a triangle shape so that the first cast-on stitch is on your left and the last cast-on stitch (with the ball of yarn attached) is on your right. Make sure that none of your stitches are twisted.

2

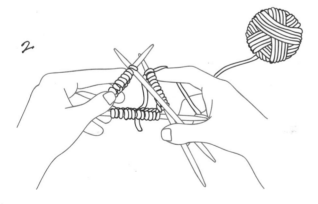

Pick up your fourth double-pointed needle and start knitting the stitches off your left needle. You're now joined in the round.

3

When you have knitted all the stitches off the left needle, that needle will become free to knit the stitches off the next needle. Keep going like this, knitting stitches off one needle and using the free needle to knit the stitches off the next, until you reach the end of your round.

Casting off on DPNs works exactly the same way as casting off on straight needles: knit two stitches, then leapfrog the first over the second. When you get to the end of a needle and there's only one stitch left, simply slip it on to the next needle and carry on casting off.

Often, a pattern will require you to start knitting using circular needles and then switch to double-pointed needles at a certain point. For example, when you knit a hat, you'll need to switch to double-pointed needles when you get near the top of the hat and the stitches become too few to fit around your circular needle. If you don't want to invest in both kinds of needles just to knit one pattern, buy the double-pointed needles and forget the circulars. You can just as easily knit the whole pattern using DPNs.

Colour Knitting

There are a number of ways to create areas of colour in your work; duplicate stitch, intarsia and Fair Isle are the most popular. Fair Isle is about as complicated as knitting gets and not for the beginner. Intarsia, however, isn't such a headache and duplicate stitch is plain easy.

Fair Isle

Fair Isle knitting is a traditional technique used to create intricate patterns with multiple strands of colour and originates from Fair Isle, a tiny island north of Scotland.

Fair Isle fabric is very pretty but, to be quite honest, I'm totally allergic to it: I just don't have the patience and I get a headache even thinking about all that twisting and trying to work so many strands of yarn at once. No, thank you very much.

But if you've been blessed with the gift of patience and do fancy giving Fair Isle a try, Alice Starmore is the lady to teach you. From what I've read about her, Starmore sounds pretty bonkers to me but she's been designing patterns since the age of five and is widely considered the doyenne of Fair Isle design and technique. At the time of writing, only one of her classic books is in print (*Alice Starmore's Book of Fair Isle Knitting*, 1988) but her patterns are available to buy (along with the yarn to make them) on her website: www.virtualyarns.com.

Intarsia

Knitting motifs into your work using a different-colour yarn – a red heart on a black scarf or a yellow lightening bolt on a blue cushion, for example – is called intarsia.

When I'm knitting gifts, I sometimes knit a tiny heart or an initial into the piece somewhere as a little secret for the recipient to find.*

When knitting intarsia, blocks of colour are worked with separate balls of yarn and there is only one active ball at any given time (unlike in Fair Isle knitting, where all the different-coloured yarns in use are carried across the back of the work). When a new colour is introduced on a row, the old colour is left hanging at the back. Because each section of colour requires you use a separate ball of yarn, if you have lots of different colours to work with, they may be easier to manage if you wind lengths of each colour yarn on to bobbins to prevent the inactive yarn becoming tangled up.

*Madame Defarge in Dickens's *A Tale of Two Cities* did something similar, although she worked the name of her enemies into her knitting while watching people being guillotined. She was evil.

The important thing to remember with intarsia is that when you change colour, you must twist the old yarn and the new yarn together so that you aren't left with ugly holes in your work. Here's how you do it.

To bring a new colour into play:

1

Insert the point of your right needle into the next stitch on your left needle as if you were going to knit (or purl) but don't actually knit the stitch. Place the new yarn across the point of the right needle from left to right with the ball end of the yarn on the right.

1

2

2

Wrap the new yarn (the ball end) around and under the old yarn and knit (or purl) a stitch in the usual way, allowing the tail end of the new colour to drop off the right needle.

To change colour in the middle of a row:

1

Twist the two different-coloured yarns together by picking up the new colour from underneath the old colour before knitting (or purling) the next stitch.

1

Duplicate Stitch

Duplicate stitch, or Swiss darning as it's sometimes called, is a great way to add a small colour motif to your work without fussing about with Fair Isle or intarsia. All you have to do is sew on top of your finished knitting, i.e., duplicate your stitches. It's colour work for cheaters.

Work out which stitches you want to duplicate and mark them with an erasable fabric pen (you don't *have* to mark them like this but it makes it a darn sight easier if you do), then:

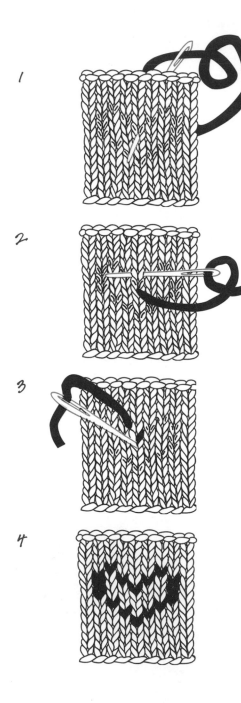

1

1

Thread a length of your contrasting colour on to a tapestry needle and insert the needle from the back of your work to the front through the bottom of a stitch (the bottom of a 'v').

2

Now insert the needle across the stitch above.

3

Insert the needle back into the bottom of the 'v' where you began. You've just duplicated a stitch.

4

Keep going like this until all the marked stitches have been doubled up. Voila – one pretty little heart!

Cabling

Cabling is actually fairly simple and used in the right way (i.e., very sparingly), it can look pretty special.

Making cables involves twisting a group of stitches by slipping them on to a cable needle and then knitting them off again in a different direction. You can hold your cable needle with the suspended stitches either at the front of your work (which will create a twist going to the left) or at the back of your work (which will send them to the right).

You only need to work the cable stitch once in a set number of rows and how many rows that is depends on the size of your cable. It's a simple formula: if you're making a four-stitch cable (C4), you'll work it once in every four rows; if you're working a six-stitch cable (C6), you'll work it once in every six rows, and so on.

Your pattern will tell you when you need to work the cable stitch and the direction will look like this: 'C6F' means you need to work the cable stitch over those six stitches with the cable needle held in front of your work; 'C6B' means you hold the cable needle to the back. Here's how you do a C6F:

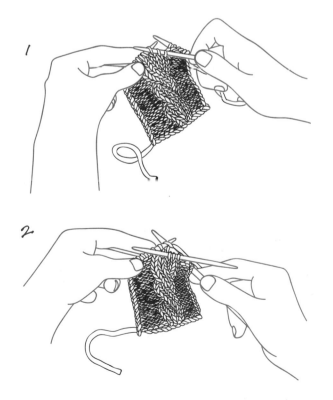

1

Slip the next 3 stitches purlwise on to your cable needle (i.e., insert your needle into the stitch as if you were going to purl, then just let them slip from one needle to the other).

2

Ignoring the stitches on the cable needle hanging down the front of your work, knit the next stitch off your left needle. Pull the yarn tight and knit the next 2 stitches.

3

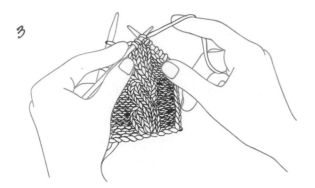

3

Now you're going to knit the stitches off your cable needle – this is where the twisting happens (and probably the shouting too, because it can be a little fiddly at first) – so go ahead and knit the first stitch, pull the yarn tight and knit the last two stitches.

Try working a cable swatch using the following pattern:

Cast on 14 stitches

Row 1: P4, k6, p4 (i.e., purl 4 stitches, knit 6 stitches, purl 4 stitches)

Row 2: K4, p6, k4

Row 3: P4, C6F (work the cable stitch as above), p4

Row 4: K4, p6, k4

Row 5: P4, k6, p4

Row 6: K4, p6, k4

Keep repeating rows 1–6 and a long twisty rope will creep up the middle of your work.

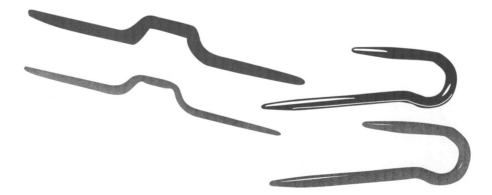

How to make buttonholes

Making a buttonhole is simple and requires you to know only how to cast off and cast on in the middle of a row (see pp. 75, 72). You'll need to know how to make buttonholes to make some of the patterns in this book, including the laptop case, baby bibs and a version of the wristwarmers with thumbholes. So here's how you do it:

1

Knit to the position of your buttonhole, then cast off the number of stitches dictated by your pattern (how many stitches you cast off will determine the length of your buttonhole). Knit to the end of the row.

2

On the next row, knit to the place where your cast-off stitches begin on the previous row. Turn your work around so that the stitches you have just knitted are on the left needle. Cast on the same number of stitches that you cast off, using the cable cast-on method shown on p. 72. Turn your work back around and knit to the end of the row.

How to make an I-cord

When I was a little girl, my Granny gave me a Knitting Nancy for my birthday (a wooden doll with nails knocked into her head and a hole running from top to bottom) and taught me how to weave yarn around and over the nails until a neat little knitted tube started to appear at the doll's feet. I never really knew what to do with all those knitted cords but now I can find no end of uses for them: drawstrings, mitten strings, hat strings, dreadlocks – the list is endless. Thanks to HRH Elizabeth Zimmermann, I no longer have to use a little wooden dolly when I need to make a knitted cord and use instead her brilliant I-cord technique. It's easy. In fact, it's so easy that EZ named it the idiot cord because it's simple enough for any idiot to do. All you need are two double-pointed needles and some yarn.

1

Cast on three stitches on to one of your double-pointed needles.

2

Knit these three stitches in the normal way.

3

Now, instead of turning your work around to knit back the other way, swap hands and slide the stitches to the other end of the needle. At this point, the needle with the stitches should be in your left hand with the ball end of the yarn hanging on the left side (it would normally be on the right).

4

Pull the yarn tight and knit across. (This is where the magic happens – pulling the yarn across from the left instead of the right forces your knitting to join in the round and make a tidy little tube.)

5

Repeat steps 4 and 5 until your I-cord is the desired length, then cast off as you normally would.

Finishing

Weaving in yarn ends and sewing up seams is seldom seen as the exciting bit of knitting. In fact, most people find it a total bore. But 'finishing', as it's called, is actually one of the most important stages in the knitting process. Casting off the last stitches on your needles is incredibly satisfying and the impulse to hurry along and finish those seams any which way you can is strong. But listen up: if you hurry this stage, there's a good chance you'll ruin your beautifully knitted thing with sloppy seaming and, after hours of labour, that's the last thing you want.

Seams

Always sew up your seams using the same yarn you knit with, unless you're using a really chunky yarn, in which case use a thinner yarn in a similar colour.

Backstitch

Sewing knitted pieces together using backstitch will create a strong, firm and bulky seam. It's not the best method to use if you need your seams to be stretchy but it's quick and really easy.

1
Place the knitted pieces to be joined together with the right sides facing each other and pin in place, making sure the rows are lined up on each side.

2
Holding the pieces with the edges to be seamed together at the top, insert your tapestry needle from back to front through both pieces at the far right-hand corner about 5mm from the top edge.

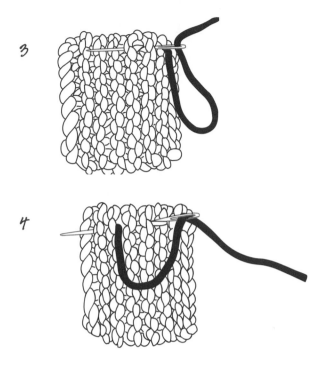

3

Insert your needle down through both pieces of fabric just along from where you first came up and then draw the needle up again about 1cm along to the left, pulling the yarn through as you go.

4

Now insert your needle back into the left side of the stitch you've just made and draw the needle up again 1cm further along to the left.

5

Repeat step 4 until you reach the end of the seam. Secure your last stitch by taking the yarn around the edge of the work and back through the final stitch.

Mattress Stitch

Mattress stitch works like magic to create an invisible seam. It's more difficult to master than backstitch but the seams won't be stiff and bulky.

Before you start working the mattress stitch, you'll need to secure your yarn. Lay the knitted pieces to be seamed next to each other, right sides facing out. Insert your tapestry needle threaded with your yarn into the bottom-right corner stitch of the left-hand piece going from front to back. Then make a figure of eight by inserting your needle through the bottom-left corner stitch of the right-hand piece going from front to back and then inserting your needle back into the corner of the left-hand piece going from front to back.

Pull the yarn tight and begin working your seam.

Joining stocking stitch pieces with mattress stitch:

1

2

To work mattress stitch on stocking stitch fabric, you'll be sewing around the little horizontal bars that run between the edge stitch and the stitch right next to it. Gently stretch your knitted piece and you'll be able to spot the bars.

1

Thread your tapestry needle under the first bar on the right-hand piece.

2

Insert the needle under the first bar on the left-hand piece.

3

Now insert the needle under the next bar up on the right-hand piece and then under the parallel bar on the left-hand piece.

Keep going like this, weaving back and forth through the parallel bars, until you reach the top. Carefully pull the yarn and watch the seams magically cosy up to one another. Secure the yarn by connecting the two top corner stitches using the figure-of-eight method you started with.

Joining garter stitch pieces with mattress stitch:

To work mattress stitch on garter stitch fabric, you'll be weaving in and out of little loops. If you look carefully, you'll see that garter stitch is made up of top loops (which look like little hills) and bottom loops (which look like valleys).

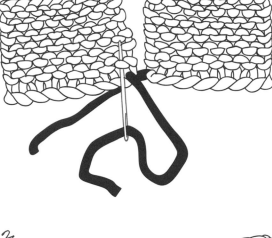

1

Thread your tapestry needle under the first bottom loop in the corner of the left-hand piece.

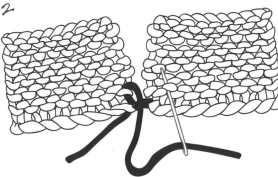

2

Insert the needle under the first top loop in the corner of the right-hand piece.

3

Now insert the needle under the next bottom loop up on the left-hand piece and then under the next top loop up on the right-hand piece.

Continue weaving through the bottom loops on the left-hand piece and the top loops on the right-hand piece until you reach the top, pulling the yarn as you go and securing with the figure-of-eight method when you get to the top.

Kitchener Stitch

Grafting creates a completely seamless join and, as Lord Kitchener intended, is most often used to close the toes of socks.

Now this is where seaming starts to get complicated. The Kitchener stitch was named for Lord Kitchener (the Secretary of State for War in the First World War, whose moustachioed face appeared on those famous 'Your Country Needs You' posters). As well as being a military hero, Kitchener was involved in a Red Cross initiative to get women knitting for the troops, and being a natty knitter himself, he contributed his own sock design with a special seamlessly 'grafted' toe that would be more comfortable for the wearer than the standard method of seaming.

Grafting creates a completely seamless join and, as Lord Kitchener intended, is most often used to close the toes of socks. It has to be done on two sets of 'live' stitches (stitches that have not yet been cast off) and there must be the same number of stitches on each needle. When it's time to graft, hold the knitted pieces to be joined with the wrong sides facing each other and the ball end of the yarn to the right on the back needle. Snip your yarn, leaving a long tail to graft with (three times the width of the seam to be knitted should do it), thread the tail of yarn on to a tapestry needle and then:

1
Insert your tapestry needle into the first stitch on the front needle as if you were going to purl, pull the yarn through and leave the stitch on the needle.

2
Now insert your tapestry needle into the first stitch on the back needle as if you were going to knit, pull the yarn through and leave the stitch on the needle.

These first two steps are 'set-up' steps and will only be done once during the process.

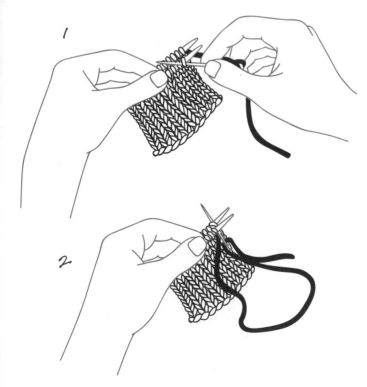

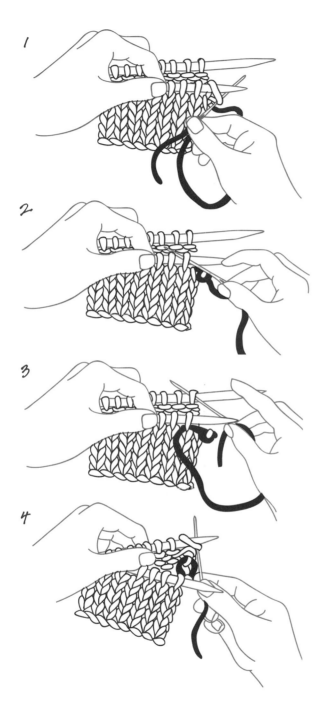

Now for the actual grafting:

1

Insert your tapestry needle into the first stitch on the *front* needle as if you were going to *knit*, pull the yarn through and let that stitch drop off the needle.

2

Insert the tapestry needle into the next stitch on the *front* needle as if you were going to *purl*, pull the yarn through but don't let it drop off the needle.

3

Insert the tapestry needle into the first stitch on the *back* needle as if you were going to *purl*, pull the yarn through and let that stitch drop off the needle.

4

Now insert the needle into the next stitch on the *back* needle as if you were going to *knit*, pull the yarn through but don't let it drop off the needle.

Repeat steps 1 to 4 until all the stitches have been joined ('grafted') together. This method of seaming isn't particularly difficult but it does require your full concentration to remember which stitch you should be working on and whether you should be inserting your needle as if to knit or to purl. So pay attention: if you get it right, you will marvel at the magically seamless edge you've just created.

Blocking

Blocking is a method of stretching and shaping your finished knitting to smooth out imperfections. No matter how neat a knitter you are, you'll always have a few lumpy bits that will need banishing. Blocking is also a good way to stretch (or shrink) your knitting to the dimensions suggested by your pattern or to make two matching pieces exactly the same size – very useful when you're making clothes.

I never used to bother with blocking but that all changed when I was making a lacy scarf for my mum. Casting the last stitches off my needles, I was really disappointed with the results: the lacy pattern I had painstakingly worked on was wonky and amateur looking, you couldn't see the intricate design and the whole scarf was sort of curling in on itself. After sulking for a few hours, I decided to give blocking a chance. I couldn't believe the difference it made: not only did the scarf lie nice and flat but it also made the lace pattern 'open up' so that the beautiful design was clearly defined.

Now, there are a number of different ways to block, some more aggressive than others. I usually use the first method described opposite, which will straighten out scarves and throws and pretty much anything else. If you need to be more aggressive in your approach, for example, if the hat you've made is a size too small, use the second method. For both methods you will need some pins (preferably long ones with big heads), a clean towel and a flat surface.

Edge Stitches

Now that you've worked up a few swatches (and you're very naughty if you haven't), you will have noticed that the side edges on those swatches have a tendency to turn out a little ugly. This doesn't matter so much when you're planning to join them to other pieces, but if you're making something where your edges will be on show, like a scarf or a blanket, you'll want them to look pretty.

There are a number of ways to tidy up your edges; the most common is to simply slip the first stitch of every row (i.e., pass the first stitch from the left-hand needle to the right without knitting it). If you do this, you'll create a lovely chain along the side and banish those wonky bumps. You could also try knitting the first stitch of every row, regardless of your stitch pattern.

Light Blocking

1

Using your hands, gently stretch your finished knitting horizontally, vertically and diagonally several times. This will even out your stitches and stretch out any lumpy bits.

2

Lay a towel down on a flat surface (the floor or a table), place your knitting on the towel and pin in place.

3

Spray the whole thing with water using a spray bottle (or the spray function on your iron) and leave it to dry overnight.

Heavy Blocking

1

Fill your sink with lukewarm water. (*Caution*: hot water does bad things to yarn so make sure the water really is lukewarm and not hot.)

2

Soak your knitting in the water for five minutes or so (you could add some gentle wool detergent at this stage if you like but make sure you rinse it properly).

3

Remove your knitting from the water and carefully squeeze some of the excess water out by rolling it in a towel.

4

Gently stretch and shape your knitting to the required size, lay it out on a clean towel and pin in place.

5

Leave to dry overnight.

Note: blocking only works on natural fibres so don't waste your time trying to straighten out anything acrylic or nylon.

Fixing Mistakes

Every beginner makes mistakes – hell, I still make a bunch of them. Although mistakes in your work can lend it a certain homemade charm, most things can easily be fixed.

Picking Up Dropped Stitches

Dropped stitches are the bane of all beginner knitters. When you're fumbling around with two hands, two needles and a load of yarn, it's all too easy to accidentally let a stitch slip off your needles while you work. The results are horrific – your work will begin to unravel, just like a ladder in your tights – but with a little patience, it can be sorted.

The first thing you need to do when you notice a stitch has been dropped is stop right where you are, carefully put your knitting down and assess the damage. Then . . .

To pick up a stitch dropped one row earlier:

1

Pick up the dropped stitch and the horizontal strand above it by inserting your right needle from front to back.

2

Insert your left needle into the back of the dropped stitch and lift it up and over the strand and off the needle (just like you would when you're passing a slipped stitch over).

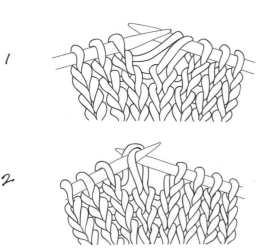

1

2

3

Transfer the stitch to the left needle by inserting the point of your left needle through the front of the stitch.

To pick up a stitch dropped several rows earlier:

The dropped stitch will make a ladder running down the front of your work and you'll need a crochet hook to sort it out.

1

Insert your crochet hook into the dropped stitch from front to back, grab the first strand of the ladder above it and pull it through the stitch.

2

Now grab the next strand of the ladder and pull that through the stitch you just made. Keep going like this until you have pulled the dropped stitch all the way up to the top.

3

Transfer the stitch from the crochet hook on to the left needle, being careful not to twist it.

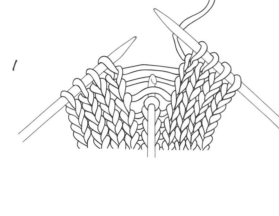

1

Unknitting

Knitting in front of the telly is one of my favourite pastimes but it's easy to lose concentration on your knitting when the action on the box gets a little too exciting, and before you know it, you've gone and knitted a load of stitches that you were meant to purl. When this happens, you can either carry on regardless and hope that no one notices *or* you can work in reverse and unknit the mistake. If only it was as easy to undo mistakes in real life . . .

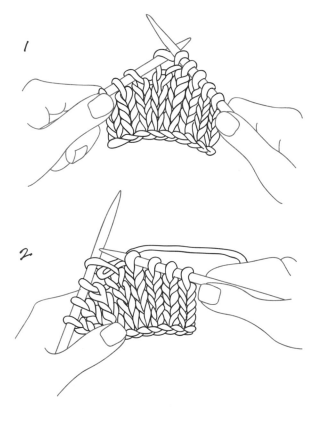

1

Insert your left needle into the stitch just below the one you just made from front to back.

2

Let the stitch drop off the right needle and pull the loose yarn through.

Keep going like this, unknitting stitches and putting them back on your left needle until you reach the point where the mistake was made.

Unravelling

When you only notice you've made a big fat mistake way after the event, it may be easier and quicker to just unravel your work to a certain point than to sit and unknit a whole load of stitches. Unravelling (actually, knitters call it 'frogging', because you have to 'rip it, rip it', but calling it this annoys me too much), is rather a drastic measure but sometimes it's the only solution.

1

Place your knitting down on a flat surface and pull your needle out.

2

Very carefully pull on the yarn so that your work begins to unravel.

3

When you reach the point where you made your mistake, take a needle a few sizes smaller than the ones you've been working with and insert it into the row of stitches one by one.

Tension Squares

Tension describes how tightly or loosely you should knit and is the term given to the number of stitches and rows you should have to the centimetre/inch knitting with the given needles, yarn and stitch pattern.

Talking about tension is totally tiresome but I'm afraid it's also totally necessary. It's very difficult to accurately work out the right number of stitches to cast on for the desired width of your knitted fabric. Those twelve tiny cast-on stitches may look like they'll yield a nice narrow piece of fabric but you could produce something way wider than you imagined. Just ask my good friend Jenny, who has been working away on the same scarf for a year now – using tiny needles and too many cast-on stitches. Jenny's scarf is an ungainly 40cm wide and no closer to being finished than it was a few months back. Her stubborn refusal to unravel and start again means her scarf will end up being a (very expensive) blanket. You can avoid this frustrating state of affairs by paying attention to tension.

Your tension describes how tightly or loosely you should knit and is the term given to the number of stitches and rows you should have to the centimetre/inch knitting with the given needles, yarn and stitch pattern. If you want your project to be the correct size and tension, you'll need to knit a tension square.

Here's how you do it: check how many stitches and rows your pattern tells you should make up a 10cm/4in square, then cast on at least six more stitches than the number given and knit away in the required pattern (garter stitch, stocking stitch or whatever) until you have knitted at least six more rows than the number given. Cast off your work and say hello to your first tension square.

To measure your tension, flatten your swatch out (pin it to the carpet if you like), lay your tape measure horizontally across your square and count the number of stitches that make up 10cm/4in. Then lay your tape measure vertically across your square and count the number of rows that make up 10cm/4in. If the number of stitches and rows per 10cm/4in exactly matches that dictated by the pattern, then bingo! You're all set to go. If it doesn't (and most likely it won't), then it's time to rethink your needle size. If the number of stitches and rows on your knitted square is less than the pattern calls for, try using needles one size smaller and, likewise, if your stats are larger than the pattern says they should be, try some larger needles.

Knitting a tension square may seem immensely boring and nerdy when all you want to do is get on and knit but trust me, it'll save you a lot of time and tears in the long run.

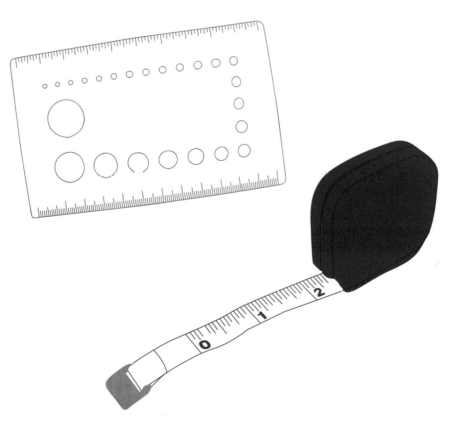

How to Read a Knitting Pattern

I won't lie to you: reading a knitting pattern can be an incredibly confusing business for the beginner knitter. Those letters and numbers will seem totally alien to you at first, but really it's just a case of learning the language.

Before you are given any actual knitting instructions, your pattern will tell you some vital information about sizes, tension and the yarn and needles you need to use.

Finished Measurements

Usually the first thing your pattern will let you know is the measurements of the finished project, e.g., a scarf might be 20cm wide, 150cm long. You may also be told what size it is, e.g., whether it's for a newborn or a three-month-old baby.

Materials

Next comes the list of materials you need to knit the thing: yarn (brand, weight and suggested colour), needles (size and type) and anything else you might need, like stitch markers or a cable needle.

Tension

This strange combination of letters and numbers will tell you how many stitches and rows make up a 10cm/4in square with the yarn and needles recommended. For example:
16 sts and 24 rows = 10cm/4in square in garter stitch with 5mm needles

means that a 10cm square of garter stitch using the yarn required and 5mm needles will be made up of 16 stitches and 24 rows. You'll need to check that these are the numbers you get when you work garter stitch using the required yarn and needles by knitting up a tension square (see pp. 100–101 for how) and adjust your needle size accordingly. Tension isn't so important when it comes to making a scarf but is vital when you're making something like a jumper or a pair of socks that really need to fit the wearer.

Knitting Instructions

It would take pages and pages to write out every single instruction of a knitting pattern in plain English, and reading all those instructions over and over again in whole sentences would give you a major migraine. Hence the reason knitting patterns are written in a series of abbreviations. Once you know what all those little abbreviations stand for (see overleaf for a list of all the ones that appear in this book and a few others that you're likely to come across once you step out into the big bad world), reading a knitting pattern is pretty simple stuff.

The best way to teach you what it's all about is to throw you right in at the deep end, so let's take a look at a few rows of a knitting pattern and break it down into simple language:

Row 1: P

Row 2: K2, *k1, p1; rep from * to last 2 sts, k2 – 20 sts

Row 3: P

Row 4: K5, k2tog, (yo, ssk) 3 times, k2tog, k5 – 18 sts

Here are the same instructions again, but this time written in plain English:

Row 1: Purl every stitch.

Row 2: Knit 2 stitches, then repeat what comes after the asterisk – in this case knit 1 stitch, then purl 1 stitch – until you have only 2 stitches left on your needle, then knit those last 2 stitches. The '20 sts' at the end of the row isn't a direction, it just means that you should have 20 stitches on your needle once you have worked that row.

Row 3: Purl every stitch.

Row 4. Knit 5 stitches, then knit 2 stitches together, then repeat the instructions that appear in parenthesis – in this case a yarn over followed by a slip, slip, knit – three times, then knit 2 stitches together and then knit the last 5 stitches. You should now have 18 stitches on your needle.

See? Not so difficult, right? I promise it's simply a case of familiarizing yourself with the abbreviations below. And after that, the world of knitting patterns is your oyster.

Sizes

Sometimes your pattern will give you instructions for multiple sizes. Instead of writing out different instructions for each size, directions for making sizes other than the smallest one will appear in parenthesis. For example, a pattern for a jumper with three different sizes may say: small (medium, large). This means that when it comes to the knitting instructions, the directions for the small size will be first and the directions for the medium and large sizes will appear in parenthesis. So your cast-on instructions might read something like this:

CO 30 (34, 38)

which would mean that for the small size you cast on 30 stitches, for the medium you cast on 34 stitches and for the large 38 stitches.

Stitch Glossary

beg: beginning

C6F: cable six front

C6B: cable six back

CC: contrasting colour (some patterns require you to use a different colour at a certain point; your contrasting colour is the one that is used the least. Your main colour will be abbreviated 'MC')

CO: cast on

dec: decrease

DPN: double-pointed needle

inc: increase

inc1: increase 1 (knit into front and back of stitch)

k: knit

KFB: knit into the front and back of the stitch (the same as inc1)

m1: make 1 increase

MC: main colour

p: purl

pm: place marker

rep: repeat

rnd: round (when knitting in the round, a row is called a round)

RS: right side (the side of the fabric that will be facing out)

skp: slip, knit, passed slipped stitch over

sl: slip

ssk: slip, slip, knit

sssk: slip, slip, slip, knit

st: stitch

st st: stocking stitch

tbl: through back loop (i.e., knit or purl into the back loop of a stitch)

tog: together

yo: yarn over

WS: wrong side

Fancy Stitch Patterns

You know how to make the most common stitch patterns – garter, stocking, rib and moss – but there are a million and one other stitch patterns to be made using a combination of knit and purl stitches and some sneaky little tricks. It's a sad state of affairs, but I know so many people who have given up knitting because they got bored of making endless garter stitch scarves but didn't feel ready to move on to making more complicated things like socks and sweaters. Experimenting with stitch patterns is the perfect way to get creative and combat the boredom while you're psyching yourself up for the more technical projects.

I am completely obsessed with stitch patterns and spend a lot of time dreaming up projects to use a newly discovered one. Below are a few of my favourites. Use them to spruce up a simple scarf or for a more fancy iPod sock. Or why not make a whole load of swatches in different stitch patterns and join them together to make a blanket? The possibilities are endless . . .

Broken Rib

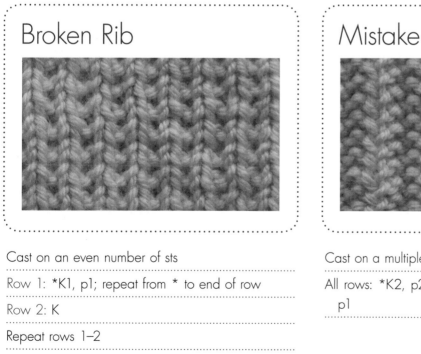

Cast on an even number of sts

Row 1: *K1, p1; repeat from * to end of row

Row 2: K

Repeat rows 1–2

Mistake Rib

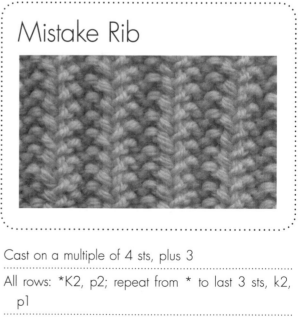

Cast on a multiple of 4 sts, plus 3

All rows: *K2, p2; repeat from * to last 3 sts, k2, p1

Lace Star Rib

Cast on a multiple of 4 sts, plus 1

Row 1: P

Row 2: K1, *yo, sl 2 knitwise–k1–p2sso, yo, k1; repeat from * to end of row

Row 3: P

Row 4: Ssk, yo, k1, *yo, sl 2 knitwise–k1–p2sso, yo, k1; repeat from * to last 2 sts, yo, k2tog

Repeat rows 1–4

Diamonds

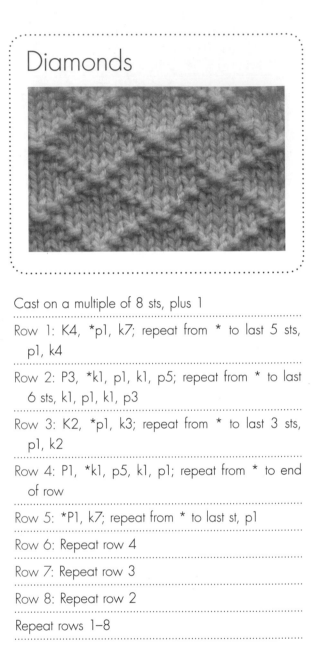

Cast on a multiple of 8 sts, plus 1

Row 1: K4, *p1, k7; repeat from * to last 5 sts, p1, k4

Row 2: P3, *k1, p1, k1, p5; repeat from * to last 6 sts, k1, p1, k1, p3

Row 3: K2, *p1, k3; repeat from * to last 3 sts, p1, k2

Row 4: P1, *k1, p5, k1, p1; repeat from * to end of row

Row 5: *P1, k7; repeat from * to last st, p1

Row 6: Repeat row 4

Row 7: Repeat row 3

Row 8: Repeat row 2

Repeat rows 1–8

Remember...

The direction to cast on a multiple of a certain number of stitches means that you need to make sure that your total number of cast-on stitches is divisible by that number. If you are then directed to 'plus' a certain number of stitches, you should cast on that extra number of stitches at the end. So if you have to cast on a 'multiple of 4 sts, plus 3' you need to cast on 12 stitches (or 16 stitches or 20, etc.) and then another 3 stitches.

Simple Eyelet

Cast on a multiple of 8 sts

Row 1: K

Row 2: P

Row 3: *K6, yo, k2tog; repeat from * to end of row

Row 4: P

Row 5: K

Row 6: P

Row 7: K2, *yo, k2tog, k6; repeat from * to last 6 sts, yo, k2tog, k4

Row 8: P

Repeat rows 1–8

Miniature Leaf Lace

Cast on a multiple of 6 sts, plus 1

Row 1: P

Row 2: K1, *k2tog, yo, k1, yo, ssk, k1; repeat from * to end of row

Row 3: P

Row 4: K2tog, *yo, k3, yo, sl 2 knitwise–k1–p2sso; repeat from * to last 5 sts, yo, k3, yo, ssk

Row 5: P

Row 6: K1, *yo, ssk, k1, k2tog, yo, k1; repeat from * to end of row

Row 7: P

Row 8: K2, *yo, sl 2 knitwise–k1–p2sso, yo, k3; repeat from * end last repeat k2

Repeat rows 1–8

Diagonal Stitch

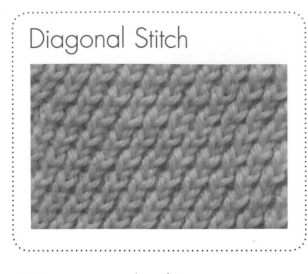

Cast on an even number of sts

Row 1: P

Row 2: *K2tog but leave sts on left needle, insert right needle between the 2 sts just knitted together, knit the first st again, then sl both sts from left needle together; repeat from * to end of row

Row 3: P

Row 4: K1, *k2tog but leave sts on left needle, insert right needle between the 2 sts just knitted together, knit the first st again, then sl both sts from left needle together; repeat from * to last st, k1

Repeat rows 1–4

Bow Stitch

Cast on a multiple of 10 sts, plus 7

Row 1: K1, *k5, sl5 purlwise with yarn in front; repeat from * to last 6 sts, k6

Row 2: P

Row 3: Repeat row 1

Row 4: P

Row 5: Repeat row 1

Row 6: P8, *insert right needle under the 3 loose strands on the front side, yarn over needle and pull up a loop (gathering loop), purl next st and sl loop over purled st, p9; repeat from * end last repeat p8

Row 7: K1, *sl5 purlwise with yarn in front, k5; repeat from * to last 6 sts, sl5 purlwise, k1

Row 8: P

Row 9: Repeat row 7

Row 10: P

Row 11: Repeat row 7

Row 12: P3, *lift 3 loose strands with gathering loop, purl next st and sl loop over purled st, p9; repeat from * end last repeat p3

Repeat rows 1–12

Baby Cables

Cast on a multiple of 4 sts, plus 2

Row 1: K2, *p2, k2; repeat from * to end of row

Row 2: P2, *k2, p2; repeat from * to end of row

Row 3: Repeat row 1

Row 4: P2, *k2tog but leave sts on left needle, insert right needle between the 2 sts just knitted together, knit the first st again, then sl both sts from left needle together, p2; repeat from * to end of row

Repeat rows 1–4

Daisy Stitch

Cast on a multiple of 4 sts, plus 1. Be careful to cast on loosely

Row 1: K

Row 2: *K1, p3tog but leave sts on left needle, yo, p same 3tog this time letting it drop off the needle; repeat from * to last st, k1

Row 3: K

Row 4: K1, p1, k1, *p3tog but leave sts on left needle, yo, p same 3tog this time letting it drop off the needle, k1; repeat from * to last 2 sts, p1, k1

Repeat rows 1–4

For more fancy stitch patterns, look no further than Barbara G. Walker's amazing *A Treasury of Knitting Patterns* (1968). The four books in the series aren't in print in the UK but I've seen them for sale in a few good yarn shops and all of them are available on US Amazon (www.amazon.com). They really are inspirational books if you're as obsessed with stitch patterns as I am. Barbara Walker was also a pretty amusing lady (and perhaps the first true feminist knitter), her mantra really hits the nail on the head: 'Don't just knit something, knit something beautiful!' Quite.

Vogue publish a series of books called 'Stitchionary', which are a nice modern alternative. There aren't as many patterns but the colour photographs give these books an edge over the black and white pictures in the Walker series.

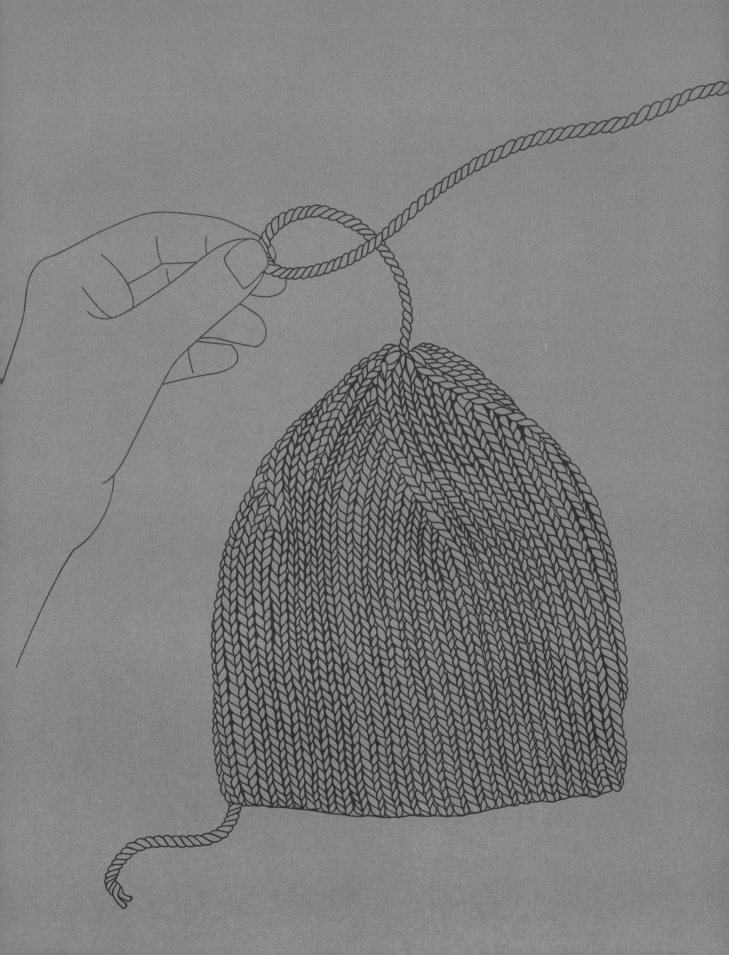

PATTERNS

The Patterns in This Book

For me, knitting is largely about creating the perfect gift for a friend or relative. Although I do knit for myself occasionally, most of my knitted creations are intended for a particular person. Even the fussiest of friends will appreciate a hand-knitted scarf or a cosy for their iPod, especially when the design and colour are matched perfectly to their tastes.

The patterns in this book are split into gift categories: gifts for girls, gifts for boys, gifts for babies, gifts for the home and novelty gifts. Of course there will be some crossovers – I happen to really love the super plain socks on p. 148 and have knitted a few pairs for myself – but you get the idea.

Not all of the designs on the following pages were born of my own genius. I spend a great deal of time on the web checking out patterns on Ravelry, chatting in the forum, keeping up with my favourite blogs and asking bloggers questions about everything from their knitting techniques to their cats. One of the reasons I love the vast global online knitting community so much is that the people, by and large, are so bloody generous – they give away their patterns, their expert advice and allow us a window into their crafting world purely for the love of the knit. I thought it would be nice to introduce you to some of the very special people I have come to know and love on my online knitting travels and so I asked a bunch of my favourite bloggers and designers to come up with a gifty pattern for you to try.

A Note on Yarns

The yarns suggested on the following pages are the ones that were used to knit the things you see in the photographs. Remember: these are just suggestions. You know how to substitute yarns (see p. 38 for a refresher) so get creative and try something a little different to make your project unique.

Patterns are rated by difficulty from the seriously easy (∗) to the challenging (∗∗∗∗∗). But don't let those five little stars scare you off. The best way to learn is to get down to it and tackle a difficult project. The first pair of socks I made taught me more in one project than anything else I have ever knitted. By the time you get to trying out the patterns in this section, I trust you will have made yourself at least a couple of simple scarves using garter stitch, moss stitch or rib stitch, which means you are ready to try something a little more taxing.

One last thing about knitting gifts: there's an old knitting myth that if you knit a strand of your own hair into everything gift you knit, you will bind the recipient to you for ever. Kind of creepy but I like the lore.

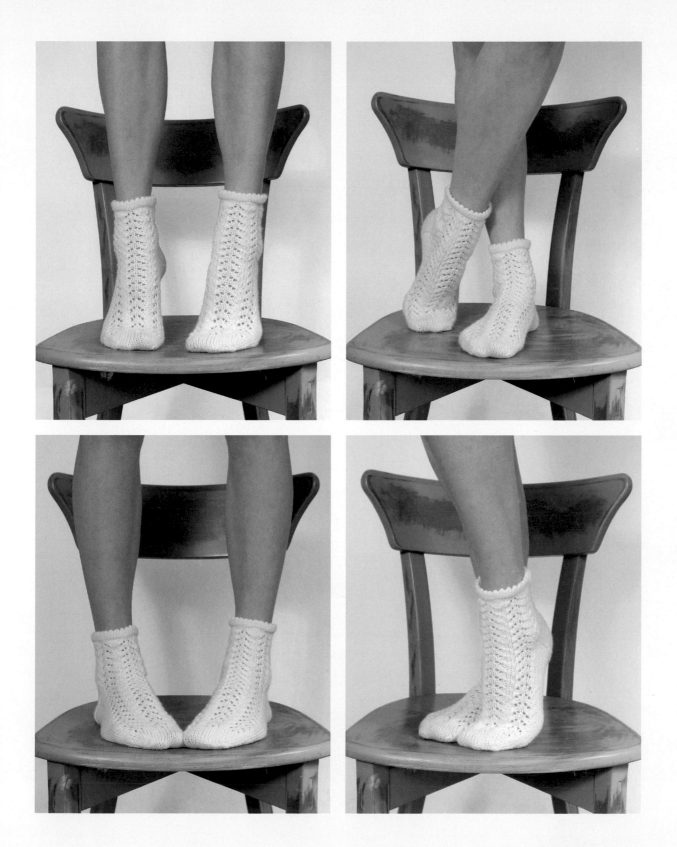

Cloud-Nine Socks

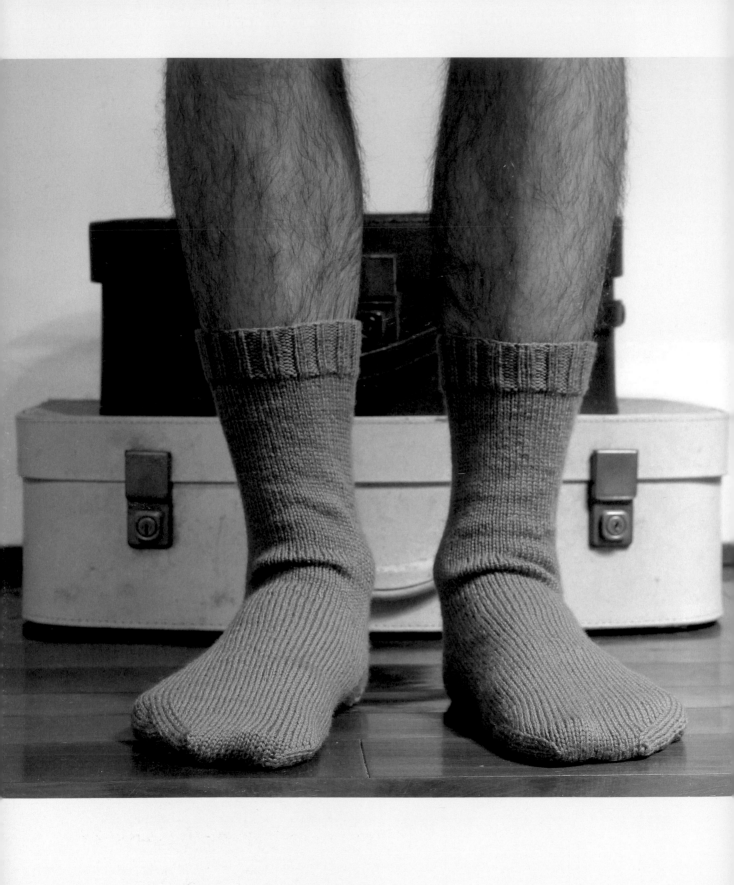

Opposite: **Basic Boy Socks** • Above: **Laptop Case**

Above: **Tea Cosy and Cafetière Cosy** • Opposite: **Honeycomb Cable Cushion**

Mortimer the Dog

Bib

Opposite: 'Born Under a Star' Blanket • Top: Mary Jane Booties • Bottom: Simple Baby Hat

Top Right: Lacy Bracelet

Bottom Right: Classic Beret

Opposite: Covered Bangles

from top to bottom: Double Moss Stitch

Bangle; Cable Bangle; Fleck Stitch Bangle

Top left: **Twisted Rib Beanie**
Top right: **Moss Stitch Tie**
Bottom left: **Moss Stitch Scarf**
Opposite: **Diagonal Knot Stitch Scarf**

Above: Chunky Cowl
Right: iPod Socks:
Dot Stitch Sock; Slip Rib Stitch Sock
Opposite page: Wristwarmers
with and without thumbholes

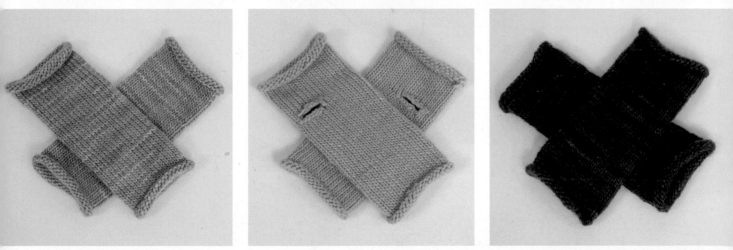

Above: **Hot Water Bottle Cover** • Top right: **Lacy Scarf** • Bottom right: **Bramble Stitch Scarf**

gifts for girls

Most of the ladies I know are suckers for soft things in beautiful colours, which make them the ideal recipients for knitted gifts. A girl can never have too many scarves and hats (especially the gorgeous scarves on pp. 130 and 131 and the classic beret on p. 136) and even your annoyingly perfect and pernickety friend will appreciate something knitted up with a luxury yarn in her favourite shade of grey. If the female in question really does only shroud herself in the kind of designer threads most of us can only dream of owning, knit her a pair of the fancy socks on p. 138: when it comes to socks, you can't get more luxury than hand-knit.

Bramble Stitch Scarf

Bramble stitch, sometimes known as trinity or cluster stitch, is one of my all time favourites. The little bumps really do look like blackberries, to my mind anyway, and are very pretty. This chunky scarf is warm and snuggly, perfect for the horrid British winter months.

Skills

Cast on: pp. 56–9

Knit: p. 62

Purl: p. 63

Purl three together (p3tog): p. 73

Cast off: pp. 66–7

Difficulty *

Finished Measurements

14cm wide, 140cm long

Materials

- Yarn: 3 x 100g Cascade Baby Alpaca Chunky in Ice Flower (559)
- Needles: 5mm

Tension

22 sts and 20 rows = 10cm/ 4in square in bramble stitch

Directions

Cast on 34 sts

Row 1: P

Row 2: *K1, (k1, p1, k1) into next st, p3tog; repeat from * to last st, k1

Row 3: P

Row 4: *K1, p3tog, (k1, p1, k1) into next st; repeat from * to last st, k1

Repeat rows 1–4 until scarf measures 140cm from cast-on edge (or desired length)

Cast off all sts

Note: the direction to '(k1, p1, k1) into next st' is worked as follows: make a knit stitch but leave the stitch on the left needle, bring your yarn to the front and purl the same stitch, again leaving it on the left needle, then take your yarn to the back and knit the stitch again, this time dropping the stitch off the left needle. You will have created three stitches from one.

Suggestions for adaptation

The yarn and needle size suggested here will yield a chunky textured scarf. If you want a more subtle texture, choose a thinner yarn, go down a few needle sizes and cast on a few more stitches. Play around knitting swatches of bramble stitch with your chosen yarn until you find the right needle size. Bramble stitch is worked over a multiple of four stitches so make sure your total number of cast-on stitches is divisible by four.

Lacy Scarf

Lace knitting isn't difficult to do and can turn a boring scarf into a work of art. This intricate and airy scarf (the stitch pattern here is called little arrowhead lace) would be perfect for the mothers and grandmothers in your life.

Skills

Cast on: pp. 56–9

Knit: p. 62

Purl: p. 63

Slip stitch (sl 1): p. 74

Slip, slip, knit (ssk): p. 74

Knit two together (k2tog): p. 73

Yarn over (yo): p. 71

Slip, slip, knit, pass two slipped stitches over (s2kp): p. 75

Cast off: pp. 66–7

Difficulty **

Finished Measurements

14cm wide, 140cm long

Materials

- Yarn: 2 x 100g Rowan Cocoon in Seascape (813)
- Needles: 7mm

Tension

7 sts and 20 rows = 10cm/4in square in little arrowhead lace stitch

Directions

Cast on 21 sts

Row 1: P

Row 2: Sl 1, k1, *yo, ssk, k1, k2tog, yo, k1; repeat from * to last st, k1

Row 3: P

Row 4: Sl 1, k2, *yo, s2kp, yo, k3; repeat from * to end of row

Repeat rows 1–4 until scarf measures 140cm from cast-on edge (or desired length)

Cast off all sts

Note: the direction to s2kp is just like a regular skp except you slip two stitches, knit one stitch, then pass those two slipped stitches over.

Suggestions for adaptation

I love lace patterns and could easily devote an entire book to all the beautiful and ancient designs I've come across. Scarves are a great way to try out new lace patterns – have a go at the miniature leaf lace pattern (see p. 107) using this chunky yarn or try working 'cheater's lace' using a laceweight yarn like Rowan's Kidsilk Haze for a much lighter, cobwebby scarf.

Chunky Cowl

The modern alternative to a scarf. These used to be called snoods in my day – cross between a scarf and a hood, geddit?

Knitted in this deliciously chunky yarn, a cowl is a useful accessory to have when it's cold outside and the wind whips your scarf off your neck faster than you can keep re-wrapping it.

Skills

Cast on: pp. 56–9

Knit: p. 62

Purl: p. 63

Slip, slip, knit (ssk): p. 74

Knit two together (k2tog): p. 73

Cast off: pp. 66–7

Mattress stitch: pp. 89–91

Difficulty *

Finished Measurements

68cm circumference at cast-on edge, 58cm circumference at cast-off edge, 28cm from cast-on edge to cast-off edge

Materials

- Yarn: 2 x 100g Blue Sky Alpaca Bulky in Wolf (1007)
- Needles: 12mm

Tension

8 sts and 12 rows = 10cm/4in square in stocking stitch

Directions

Cast on 56 sts

Row 1: K

Row 2: P

Repeat rows 1–2 five more times

Row 13: K1, ssk, k to last 3 sts, k2tog, k1 – 54 sts

Row 14: P

Row 15: K1, ssk, k to last 3 sts, k2tog, k1 – 52 sts

Row 16: P

Row 17: K1, ssk, k to last 3 sts, k2tog, k1 – 50 sts

Row 18: P

Row 19: K1, ssk, k to last 3 sts, k2tog, k1 – 48 sts

Row 20: P

Row 21: K1, ssk, k to last 3 sts, k2tog, k1 – 46 sts

Row 22: P

Row 23: K

Row 24: P

Repeat rows 23–4 three more times

Cast off all sts

Sew up seam using mattress stitch

Suggestions for adaptation

Plain stocking stitch is perfect for showing off this lovely chunky yarn but for a more dramatic effect, try moss stitch (moss stitch uses up more yarn so you'll need to buy an extra ball). Or make the cowl double the length so that it can be wrapped around your neck twice for extra warmth: cast on 140 stitches (standard straight needles won't be long enough to accommodate this many stitches so you'll have to invest in a 12mm circular needle and just use it as you would a pair of straights) and knit in stocking stitch for 30 rows. You won't need to bother with the decreases because the cowl doesn't need to fit snugly against your neck when it's doubled over).

Wristwarmers

Not as pointless as you might at first think: these legwarmers for the wrists will keep you warmer than you would expect, and are very useful for stopping your hands freezing up if you work in an office with over-enthusiastic air-conditioning like I do. Plus they look great teamed with coats or cardigans with cropped sleeves.

Although you're knitting with four needles here, this pattern could not be easier. There's no shaping to be done and all you need to know is how to make knit stitches, so this is the perfect project to try if you're ready to venture into the exciting (and it *is* exciting, not scary, remember) world of knitting in the round but aren't quite prepared to tackle your first pair of socks. Don't be scared, it really isn't hard . . .

Below are directions for two different versions of these wristwarmers: one with thumbholes and one without.

Skills
Cast on: pp. 56–9
Knit: p. 62
Knit in the round: pp. 78–81
Cast off in the middle of a round: p. 75
Cast on in the middle of a round: p. 72
Cast off: pp. 66–7

Difficulty ✳✳

Finished Measurements
17cm circumference (unstretched), 22cm long (flat measurement – the edges will curl in a little so expect to lose about 1cm on each edge)

Tension
22 sts and 30 rows = 10cm/4in square in stocking stitch

Directions

● Simple Wristwarmers

Cast on 35 sts. Divide sts on to three needles and join for working in the rnd, being careful not to twist the sts

Work st st (by knitting all sts every rnd) until piece measures 22cm from cast-on edge

Cast off all stitches loosely

Work second wristwarmer the same as the first

● Wristwarmers with Thumbhole

Cast on 35 sts. Divide sts on to three needles and join for working in the rnd, being careful not to twist the sts

Work st st (by knitting all sts every rnd) until piece measures 15cm from cast-on edge

Next rnd: K3, cast off 7 sts, k to end of rnd

Next rnd: K3, turn and, using cable cast-on method, cast-on 7 sts, turn and knit to end of rnd

Carry on working st st until piece measures 22cm from cast-on edge

Cast off all sts loosely

Work second wristwarmer the same as the first

Materials

- Yarn: 1 x Malabrigo Worsted (one skein of yarn will make two pairs of wristwarmers), in Tortuga, Pigeon or Damask
- Needles: 4.5mm double-pointed

Suggestions for adaptation

This pattern is easy to adapt for yarns of different thickness. Invest in a set of needles in the size your yarn label suggests and then play around with your number of cast-on stitches until your tube fits your wrist. Easy.

You could also adapt the pattern to make legwarmers: choose a chunkier yarn, then just cast on a few more stitches to make a bigger tube and add a few more rounds to make them longer.

Classic Beret

Let me introduce you to the designer of this sophisticated beret: Susan Sharp. Susan is a primary school teacher but in her spare time she runs the fantastic little yarn sanctuary Sharp Works in southeast London with her daughter, Rose (see p. 164 and p. 174 for Rose's beautiful designs).

Skills

Cast on: pp. 56–9

Knit: p. 62

Purl: p. 63

Knit in the round: pp. 78–81

Increase one (inc1): p. 70

Slip, knit, pass slipped stitch over (skp): p. 75

Difficulty ✳✳✳

Finished Measurements

26cm diameter on top of hat

Materials

- Yarn: 2 x 50g Rowan Felted Tweed Aran in Dusty (728)
- Needles: 5mm double-pointed
- Stitch marker

Tension

18 sts and 24 rows = 10cm/4in square in stocking stitch

Directions

Cast on 80 sts. Divide sts on to three needles. Join, being careful not to twist the sts and place marker to indicate beginning of rnd

● Ribbing

Rnds 1–6: *K1, p1; repeat from * to end of rnd

● Increase Rounds

Rnd 7: *K9, inc1; repeat from * to end of rnd – 88 sts   99

Rnd 8: K

Rnd 9: *K10, inc1; repeat from * to end of rnd – 96 sts

Rnd 10: K

Rnd 11: *K11, inc1; repeat from * to end of rnd – 104 sts

Rnd 12: K

Rnd 13: *K12, inc1; repeat from * to end of rnd – 112 sts

Rnd 14: K

Rnd 15: *K13, inc1, repeat from * to end of rnd – 120 sts

Rnd 16: K

Rnd 17: *K14, inc1; repeat from * to end of rnd – 128 sts

Rnd 18: K

Rnd 19: *K15, inc1; repeat from * to end of rnd – 136 sts

Rnds 20–23: K

● Decrease Rounds

Rnd 24: *K15, skp; repeat from * to end of rnd – 128 sts

Rnd 25: K

Rnd 26: *K14, skp; repeat from * to end of rnd – 120 sts

Rnd 27: K

Rnd 28: *K13, skp; repeat from * to end of rnd – 112 sts

Rnd 29: K

Rnd 30: *K12, skp; repeat from * to end of rnd – 104 sts

Rnd 31: K

Rnd 32: *K11, skp; repeat from * to end of rnd – 96 sts

Rnd 33: K

Rnd 34: *K10, skp; repeat from * to end of rnd – 88 sts

Rnd 35: K

Rnd 38: *K9, skp; repeat from * to end of rnd – 80 sts

Rnd 39: K

Rnd 40: *K8, skp; repeat from * to end of rnd – 72 sts

Rnd 41: K

Rnd 42: *K7, skp; repeat from * to end of rnd – 64 sts

Rnd 43: K

Rnd 44: *K6, skp; repeat from * to end of rnd – 56 sts

Rnd 45: K

Rnd 46: *K5, skp; repeat from * to end of rnd – 48 sts

Rnd 47: K

Rnd 48: *K4, skp; repeat from * to end of rnd – 40 sts

Rnd 49: K

Rnd 50: *K3, skp; repeat from * to end of rnd – 32 sts

Rnd 51: K

Rnd 52: *K2, skp; repeat from * to end of rnd – 24 sts

Rnd 53: K

Rnd 54: *K1, skp; repeat from * to end of rnd – 16 sts

Rnd 55: K

Rnd 56: *Skp; repeat from * to end of rnd – 8 sts

Cut yarn leaving a 10cm tail and thread on to a tapestry needle.
Insert the tapestry needle through each of the sts, removing them
from the needle as you go. Pull the yarn tight to close up the top of
the hat and weave the yarn end in underneath

Suggestions for adaptation

For a cutesy version of this beret, attach a pom-pom to the top of the hat. Here's how to make one:

1 Cut out two circles of the same size from some stiff card (the larger your circles, the larger your pom-pom).

2 Make a hole in the middle of each card about half the size of the circle itself.

3 Place the circles on top of each other and wind your yarn around the cards through the hole in the middle again and again until there isn't room to wind any more.

4 Using a pair of scissors, cut around the circumference of the circles, snipping the loops of yarn.

5 Wrap a piece of yarn around the middle of your pom-pom, between the two pieces of card, tie a knot and pull it tight.

6 Pull the pieces of card away from the pom-pom (you may have to cut them to do this) and voila! There you have your pom-pom.

Attach the pom-pom to the top of your hat using the same yarn. And don't stop here with the pom-poms - sew one to each end of a scarf or make a couple of teeny ones to attach to the back of your socks. Pom-poms are cute - don't let anyone tell you otherwise.

Cloud-Nine Socks

Plenty of knitters are obsessed with knitting socks but until recently I never really understood the fascination – I always assumed it would be difficult and it seemed a total waste of time to make the effort for something that would only be hidden under my trousers. But, drooling over the photographs on Jane Brocket's blog of the pretty socks she makes, I decided it was time to take the plunge. And I'm so glad I did because not only is it a damn sight easier than I ever could have imagined, it's also really fun: there's something so satisfying about watching a sock magically grow on your needles.

When I asked Jane how she came to fall in love with knitting socks, I was surprised to hear she was a fairly recent convert too: 'I'd been knitting for years, nay decades, before I attempted my first sock. Held back by the belief that a knitter must have to possess almost mystical powers to be able to knit on such tiny double-pointed needles, count rows while knitting a spiral, turn heels (gasp), and effect a neat finish at the toe, I decided that sock knitting was beyond me.'

Inspired by a friend who managed to produce a beautiful pair of red and blue striped socks while talking *and* drinking wine, Jane decided to face her fears and have a go herself: 'I discovered that not only was it just like following any other pattern, it was also easy (I chose a very simple pattern that came free with a ball of sock yarn). I didn't have to deal with complicated heel-turning or Kitchener stitches because I simply followed the instructions which spelled out everything I needed to do without using fancy stitch language.'

The thought of having to 'turn a heel' and 'graft a toe' is enough to put most people off knitting socks. But really, if you stick to a simple pattern with clear instructions, you'll be turning a heel and grafting a toe without even realizing you're doing it.

Jane was more than pleased with the results of her first foray into sock knitting: 'I couldn't believe just how lovely a hand-knitted sock could look and feel. They are soft and cosy and, because I use all sorts of self-striping yarns which take away the need for colour-changes and complex patterns, they also look great.'

You should listen to this lady – she really does know what she's talking about. And if you find yourself on her blog (www.yarnstorm.blogs.com) and aren't immediately inspired to knit a pair for yourself, there's something seriously wrong with you.

These gorgeously fancy socks were designed by spinner extraordinaire Debbie Orr. Knitting since her mum taught her at the age of four, Debbie now runs the wonderful online shop Skein Queen (see p. 196) from her home in Berkshire and is lucky enough to make a living from her passion for yarn and colour.

As sock patterns go, these are more challenging than the basic pattern you'll find on p. 148 (and it might be a good idea to knit a pair of those first) but don't let that put you off. Socks as pretty as these ones really are worth the effort.

Skills

Cast on: pp. 56–9

Knit: p. 62

Purl: p. 63

Knit in the round: pp. 78–81

Slip stitch (sl 1): p. 74

Yarn over (yo): p. 71

Knit two together (k2tog):
  p. 73

Purl two together (p2tog):
  p. 73

Slip, slip, knit (ssk): p. 74

Slip, knit, pass slipped stitch
  over (skp): p. 75

Picking up stitches along a
  selvedge: p. 77

Kitchener stitch: pp. 92–3

Difficulty *****

Size

To fit an average women's foot

Finished Measurements

20cm from cuff to heel,
20cm from heel to toe,
unstretched

Materials

- Yarn: 1 x 100g ball of Skein
  Queen Plushness
- Needles: 3mm double-
  pointed
- Stitch markers

Tension

30 sts and 38 rows = 10cm/
4in square in stocking stitch

Directions

• Picot Edge

Cast on 54 sts. Divide sts on to four needles. Join, being careful not
  to twist the sts and place marker to indicate beginning of rnd

Rnds 1–5: K

Rnd 6: *Yo, k2tog; repeat from * to end of rnd

Rnds 7–12: K

Fold top of cuff in half with right side facing out so that holes created
  by the yarn overs form little peaks. Now here's the tricky bit: insert
  your left needle (the first needle in the rnd) into the middle of the
  first cast-on stitch; now knit tog with the first st on your left needle
  (as if you were doing a k2tog). Keep going like this, picking up
  cast-on sts and knitting them tog with the sts on your needle to the
  end of the rnd

• Cuff

Rnd 1: K

Rnd 2: K

Rnd 3: *Skp, k2, yo, k1, yo, k2, k2tog; repeat from * to end of rnd

Rnd 4: K

Rnd 5: *K1, skp, yo, k3, yo, k2tog, k1; repeat from * to end of rnd

Repeat rnds 1–5 six more times

• Heel Flap

Knit 27 sts on to one needle, turn work so wrong side is facing. You
  will now be working back and forth across these 27 sts

Row 1: Sl 1, p to end of row

Row 2: *Sl 1, k1; repeat from * to last st, k1

Repeat rows 1–2 sixteen more times

Next row: Sl 1, p to end of row

Continues on next page

● Heel Shaping

Here comes the 'scary' bit: you'll be working back and forth on a small number of sts, leaving sts unworked on either side of your row and gradually bringing those unworked sts back into play. This is how you shape the heel. It feels a little odd and counterintuitive at first but it isn't difficult.

Row 1: Sl 1, k14, ssk, k1, turn (leave remaining 9 sts on other needle)

Row 2: Sl 1, p5, p2tog, p1, turn (leave remaining 8 sts on other needle)

Row 3: Sl 1, k6, ssk, k1, turn (here you'll begin to bring the unworked sts back into play)

Row 4: Sl 1, p7, p2tog, p1, turn

Row 5: Sl 1, k8, ssk, k1, turn

Row 6: Sl 1, p9, p2tog, p1, turn

Row 7: Sl 1, k10, ssk, k1, turn

Row 8: Sl 1, p11, p2tog, p1, turn

Row 9: Sl 1, k12, ssk, k1, turn

Row 10: Sl 1, p13, p2tog, p1, turn

Row 11: Sl 1, k14, ssk

You should now have 16 sts on your needle

● Gusset

With new needle, pick up 17 sts up side of heel flap, place marker

With new needle, knit 27 sts across cuff, place marker

With new needle, pick up 17 sts down other side of heel flap

You should now have a total of 77 sts on four needles

Rnd 1: K to within 3 sts of first marker, k2tog, k1, slip marker, k to next marker, slip marker, k1, ssk, k to end of rnd – 75 sts

Rnd 2: K to first marker, slip marker, *skp, k2, yo, k1, yo, k2, k2tog; repeat from * to next marker, slip marker, k to end of rnd

Rnd 3: K to within 3 sts of first marker, k2tog, k1, slip marker, k to next marker, slip marker, k1, ssk, k to end of rnd – 73 sts

Rnd 4: K to first marker, slip marker, *k1, skp, yo, k3, yo, k2tog, k1; repeat from * to next marker, slip marker, k to end of rnd

Rnd 5: K to within 3 sts of first marker, k2tog, k1, slip marker, k to next marker, slip marker, k1, ssk, k to end of rnd – 71 sts

Rnd 6: K to end of rnd

Rnd 7: K to within 3 sts of first marker, k2tog, k1, slip marker, *skp, k2, yo, k1, yo, k2, k2tog; repeat from * to next marker, slip marker, k1, ssk, k to end of rnd – 69 sts

Rnd 8: K to end of rnd

Rnd 9: K to within 3 sts of first marker, k2tog, k1, slip marker, *k1, skp, yo, k3, yo, k2tog, k1; repeat from * to next marker, slip marker, k1, ssk, k to end of rnd – 67 sts

Rnd 10: K to end of rnd

Rnd 11: K to within 3 sts of first marker, k2tog, k1, slip marker, k to next marker, slip marker, k1, ssk, k to end of rnd – 65 sts

Rnd 12: K to first marker, slip marker, *skp, k2, yo, k1, yo, k2, k2tog; repeat from * to next marker, slip marker, k to end of rnd

Rnd 13: K to within 3 sts of first marker, k2tog, k1, slip marker, k to next marker, slip marker, k1, ssk, k to end of rnd – 63 sts

Rnd 14: K to first marker, slip marker, *k1, skp, yo, k3, yo, k2tog, k1; repeat from * to next marker, slip marker, k to end of rnd

Rnd 15: K to within 3 sts of first marker, k2tog, k1, slip marker, k to next marker, slip marker, k1, ssk, k to end of rnd – 61 sts

Rnd 16: K to end of rnd

Rnd 17: K to within 3 sts of first marker, k2tog, k1, slip marker, *skp, k2, yo, k1, yo, k2, k2tog; repeat from * to next marker, slip marker, k1, ssk, k to end of rnd – 59 sts

Rnd 18: K to end of rnd

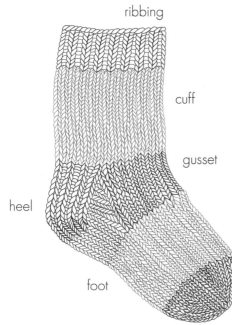

ribbing

cuff

gusset

heel

foot

toe

Continues on next page

Rnd 19: K to within 3 sts of first marker, k2tog, k1, slip marker, *k1, skp, yo, k3, yo, k2tog, k1; repeat from * to next marker, slip marker, k1, ssk, k to end of rnd – 57 sts

Rnd 20: K to end of rnd

Rnd 21: K to within 3 sts of first marker, k2tog, k1, slip marker, k to next marker, slip marker, k1, ssk, k to end of rnd – 55 sts

● Foot

Rnd 1: K to first marker, slip marker, *skp, k2, yo, k1, yo, k2, k2tog; repeat from * to next marker, slip marker, k to end of rnd

Rnd 2: K to end of rnd

Rnd 3: K to first marker, slip marker, *k1, skp, yo, k3, yo, k2tog, k1; repeat from * to next marker, slip marker, k to end of rnd

Rnds 4–5: K to end of rnd

Repeat rnds 1–5 five more times or until foot measures 3.5 cm less than required length

Next rnd: K to within 2 sts of first marker, k2tog – 54 sts

First marker now indicates beginning of rnd

● Toe Shaping

Rnd 1: K1, ssk, k to within 3 sts of next marker, k2tog, k1, slip marker, k1, ssk, k to last 3 sts, k2tog, k1 – 50 sts

Rnd 2: K to end of rnd

Repeat rnds 1–2 three more times

You should now have 38 sts on your needles

Next rnd: K

Next rnd: K1, ssk, k to within 3 sts of next marker, k2tog, k1, slip marker, k1, ssk, k to last 3 sts, k2tog, k1 – 34 sts

Next rnd: K1, ssk, k to within 3 sts of next marker, k2tog, k1, slip marker, k1, ssk, k to last 3 sts, k2tog, k1 – 30 sts

Divide remaining sts onto two needles and sew up seam using Kitchener stitch

Suggestions for adaptation

If the picot edge on these socks is a pretty step too far, ditch it in favour of a simple rib edge. Cast on 54 sts, then work in a k1, p1 rib for 8 rnds, before knitting the cuff and the rest of the pattern exactly as above.

Although Debbie's very own yarn is the perfect choice for these heavenly socks, you could just as well knit them up using any 4-ply yarn. Try a self-patterning sock yarn for a more dramatic effect or a plain-colour 4-ply like Rowan Cashsoft.

Gifts for Boys

The men in my life are notoriously impossible to please when it comes to presents. The thing to remember when knitting for men is that they don't like change (this may explain why my fussy brother has no fewer than thirty-eight plain white t-shirts). So don't go knitting a bright-red scarf for a guy who never leaves the house in a shade more interesting than beige. Take a look at his wardrobe – if he dresses himself exclusively in navy blue, black and forest green, pick a yarn that fits with his colour scheme. You should also consider the content of your yarn. If the man in question isn't quite the metrosexual who spends his weekends lovingly hand-washing his cashmere cardigans, I wouldn't advise you knit him a pair of hand-wash-only socks.

If you're brave enough to knit something for your boyfriend, choose your pattern wisely. One of the most well-known myths about knitting is the sweater curse. As the saying goes, you should never knit your boyfriend a sweater, otherwise you'll be sure to break up. Brutal. Although my ma knitted my old man a tasty Aran sweater before they were married and they've just celebrated their thirty-ninth anniversary, so it's probably a load of old twaddle. But it's better to be safe than sorry so stick to knitting scarves, hats, socks and ties for your beau.

Moss Stitch Scarf

I love, love, love moss stitch and have to work hard to resist the urge to knit everything in those pretty little bumps. It's really easy to do and creates a simple, sophisticated texture that's just the thing for a man's scarf. This version of the classic moss stitch scarf is bold and chunky but you could easily adapt it for the more sophisticated gent (see below).

Skills

Cast on: pp. 56–9

Knit: p. 62

Purl: p. 63

Cast off: pp. 66–7

Difficulty *

Finished Measurements

16cm wide, 170cm long

Materials

- Yarn: 2 x 100g balls of Rowan Big Wool in Smoky (007)
- Needles: 12mm

Tension

7 sts and 13 rows = 10cm/4in square in moss stitch

Directions

Cast on 13 sts

All rows: *K1, p1 repeat from * to end of row

Work in moss stitch until scarf measures 170cm from cast-on edge (or desired length)

Cast off all sts

Suggestions for adaptation

A moss stitch scarf knitted with an Aran-weight yarn would also be a handsome thing. Using the needles suggested by your chosen yarn, cast on the number of stitches required to make your scarf as wide or as narrow as you like.

Diagonal Knot Stitch Scarf

For the slightly more sophisticated male, this scarf was inspired by the beautiful designer men's scarves I find myself eyeing up every winter in the menswear section of Liberty. Diagonal knot stitch is a beautifully textured stitch that looks intricate and striking but it isn't difficult to work.

Skills

Cast on: pp. 56–9
Knit: p. 62
Purl: p. 63
Slip stitch (sl 1): p. 74
Purl three together: p. 73
Cast off: pp. 66–7

Difficulty **

Finished Measurements

12cm wide, 170 cm long

Materials

- Yarn: 5 x 50g balls of Rowan Cashsoft Aran in Thunder (014)
- Needles: 5mm

Tension

30 sts and 20 rows = 10cm/4in square in diagonal knot stitch

Directions

Cast on 36 sts

Row 1: Sl 1, k

Row 2: Sl 1, *MK; repeat from * to last 2 sts, p2

Row 3: Sl 1, k

Row 4: Sl 1, p2, *MK; repeat from * to last 3 sts, p3

Row 5: Sl 1, k

Row 6: Sl 1, p1 *MK; repeat from * to last stitch, p1

Repeat rows 1–6 until scarf measures 170cm (or desired length)

Cast off all sts

Note: to work the MK (which is an abbreviation for 'make', though this differs from pattern to pattern), purl three together but leave the stitches on the left needle, yarn over, then purl the same three together again.

Suggestions for adaptation

Using needles of this size keeps the stitches close together to create a flat scarf. To open up the lace aspect of this stitch pattern, go up a few needle sizes. Or try knitting it up with a chunky yarn and some fat needles (Rowan Big Wool with 12cm needles would work well) for a thicker version.

Twisted Rib Beanie

This pattern, designed by Juju Vail, uses an alternative version of the basic 1x1 rib. Juju is an all-round crafty genius, she lives in London with her husband and two children.

Difficulty **

Finished Measurements

40cm circumference

Materials

- Yarn: 1 x 100g Rowan Pure Wool Aran in Marine (683)
- Needles: 5mm double-pointed
- Stitch markers

Tension

24 sts and 26 rows = 10cm/4in square in twisted-rib stitch

Suggestions for adaptation

This pattern can be adapted to feature a roll-up bottom for a fisherman style hat. Just knit an extra 6cm in twisted rib stitch before you get to the decrease rows.

Directions

Note: twisted rib stitch is made by knitting into the back loop of all knit stitches instead of the front. Purl the purls as normal.

Cast on 105 sts. Divide sts on to four needles. Join, being careful not to twist the sts and place marker to indicate beginning of rnd

Rnd 1: *K1, p1; repeat from * to last st, k last st tog with 1st st of rnd 2 – 104 sts

Continue working k1, p1 rib st on every rnd until piece measures 11cm from cast-on edge

● Decrease Rounds

Continue in k1, p1 twisted rib pattern for one more rnd, placing a marker after every 26 sts

Rnd 1: Ssk, *k1, p1; repeat from * to first marker, slip marker, ssk, *k1, p1; repeat from * to next marker, slip marker, ssk, *k1, p1; repeat from * to next marker, slip marker, ssk, *k1, p1; repeat from * to end of rnd – 100 sts

Rnd 2: Ssk, *p1, k1; repeat from * to first marker, slip marker, ssk, *p1, k1; repeat from * to next marker, slip marker, ssk, *p1, k1; repeat from * to next marker, slip marker, ssk, *p1, k1; repeat from * to end of rnd – 96 sts

Repeat rnds 1–2 nine more times

You should now have 24 sts remaining

Cut yarn leaving a 10cm tail and thread on to a tapestry needle. Insert the tapestry needle through each of the sts, removing them from the needle as you go. Pull the yarn tight to close up the top of the hat and weave the yarn end in

Moss Stitch Tie

Ah, moss stitch. I just can't get enough of it. This retro tie was inspired by the silky knitted beauties you can buy in the luxury menswear shops on Jermyn Street in London. Those expensive ties are machine-knitted but their texture is very similar to that of moss stitch.

Skills

Cast on: pp. 56–9
Knit: p. 62
Purl: p. 63
Slip, slip, knit (ssk): p. 74
Knit two together (k2tog): p. 73
Increase one (inc1): p. 72
Cast off: pp. 66–7

Difficulty *

Finished Measurements

4cm wide (front), 120cm long

Materials

- Yarn: 1 x 50g Rowan Cotton Glace in Blood Orange (445)
- Needles: 3.25mm

Tension

25 sts and 40 rows = 10cm/4in square in moss stitch

Directions

Cast on 9 sts

All rows: K1, p1

Work moss stitch every row until piece measures 52cm from cast-on edge

● Decrease

Row 1: Ssk, k1, p1, k1, p1, k1, k2tog – 7 sts

Row 2: P1, k1

Row 3: Ssk, p1, k1, p1, k2tog – 5 sts

Work moss stitch (k1, p1) until piece measures 90cm from cast-on edge

● Increase

Row 1: Inc1, p1, k1, p1, inc1 – 7 sts

Work moss stitch (this time p1, k1) until piece measures 120cm from cast-on edge

Cast off all sts

Suggestions for adaptation

Use a thinner yarn for a tighter-weave fabric that's better suited to a suit-wearer than a trend-setter. Just cast on a few more stitches (making sure the total is an uneven number) and then knit away as above.

Basic Boy Socks

Rachael Matthews is testament to the fact that socks can be the perfect gift for a man. Once upon a time, Rachael met a man who lived on a boat with no phone and no internet access (a rare breed these days). She liked the cut of his jib and wanted to let him know, so she knitted him a pair of socks, stuffed them inside a glass bottle and let them float down the river for him to fish out. Needless to say, he was so impressed he asked her out.

Jane Brocket, sock-knitting pro, gives us her top five tips:

1 Select a super-easy pattern to begin with.

2 Bamboo double-pointed needles are the best for knitting socks. Use slightly smaller needles than those suggested by your yarn to create a tight-knit fabric that will make your socks last longer.

3 Pick a yarn with a percentage of nylon or acrylic (25 per cent should do it) as this will make your socks hard-wearing. Pure wool is a lovely thing but isn't very durable when it comes to socks.

4 Make things interesting by using self-patterning yarns which are carefully calculated to create stripes and patterns all by themselves. Yarns by Regia, Opal, Schoppel Woolle and Trekking are all great. There is a wealth of good internet sellers with a huge variety of sock yarns. Check out Modern Knitting (www.modernknitting.co.uk), Web of Wool (www.webof-wool.co.uk) and Get Knitted (www.getknitted.com).

5 If you want the stripes or patterns to match in a pair of socks, be sure to start at exactly the same point in the repeat pattern of a self-patterning yarn. This will become clear once you have knitted the first sock. Alternatively, enjoy a little randomness in your stripes.

As sock patterns go, this one is about as simple as it gets so this is the perfect place to start your love affair with sock knitting. Once you've knitted a pair for every man in your life, I can guarantee you'll be itching to knit a pair of socks for yourself – see p. 150 for how to adapt this pattern for the more dainty foot or turn to p. 138 for a girlier version.

There's an old knitting myth that says if you don't cast on your second sock as soon as you finish the first, you'll never complete the damn things. If only we were all as resourceful as Anna Makarovna in *War and Peace*, who was somehow able to knit two socks at once. I have no idea how the hell you do this or whether it's even possible, so probably best to stick to just one for now.

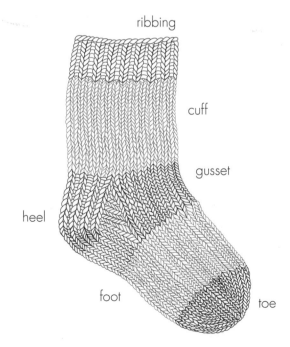

ribbing

cuff

gusset

heel

foot

toe

Skills

Cast on: pp. 56–9

Knit: p. 62

Purl: p. 63

Knit in the round: pp. 78–81

Slip stitch (sl 1): p. 74

Knit two together (k2tog):
    p. 73

Purl two together (p2tog):
    p. 73

Slip, slip, knit (ssk): p. 74

Picking up stitches along a
    selvedge: p. 77

Kitchener stitch: pp. 92–3

Difficulty *****

Size

To fit an average man's foot

Finished Measurements

25cm from cuff to heel, 24cm
from heel to toe, unstretched

Materials

- Yarn: 2 x 50g balls of Rowan
  Cashsoft 4-ply in Bluebottle
  (449)
- Needles: 3mm double-pointed
- Stitch markers

Tension

30 sts and 40 rows = 10cm/4in
square in stocking stitch

Directions

● Ribbing

Cast on 68 sts. Divide sts on to three needles. Join, being careful not to twist the sts and place marker to indicate beginning of rnd

Rnds 1–14: *K2, p2; repeat from * to end of rnd

● Cuff

Rnds 1–50: K

● Heel Flap

Knit 17 sts, turn work so wrong side is facing

Row 1: Sl 1, p33, turn (you will now be working back and forth across these 34 sts)

Row 2: Sl 1, k33, turn

Repeat rows 1–2 sixteen more times

Remember: when slipping stitches on their own (i.e., when you're not decreasing), you should always slip purlwise.

● Heel Shaping

To shape the heel, you'll be working back and forth on a small number of sts, leaving sts unworked on either side of your row and gradually bringing those unworked sts back into play.

Row 1: Sl 1, p18, p2tog, p1, turn (leave remaining 12 sts on other needle)

Row 2: Sl 1, k5, ssk, k1, turn (leave remaining 12 sts on other needle)

Row 3: Sl 1, p6, p2tog, p1, turn (here you'll begin to bring the unworked sts back into play)

Row 4: Sl 1, k7, ssk, k1, turn

Row 5: Sl 1, p8, p2tog, p1, turn

Row 6: Sl 1, k9, ssk, k1, turn

Row 7: Sl 1, p10, p2tog, p1, turn

Row 8: Sl 1, k11, ssk, k1, turn

Continues on next page

Row 9: Sl 1, p12, p2tog, p1, turn

Row 10: Sl 1, k13, ssk, k1, turn

Row 11: Sl 1, p14, p2tog, p1, turn

Row 12: Sl 1, k15, ssk, k1, turn

Row 13: Sl 1, p16, p2tog, p1, turn

Row 14: Sl 1, k17, ssk, k1, turn

You should now have 20 sts on your needle

● Gusset

With new needle, pick up 17 sts up side of heel flap, place marker

With new needle, knit 34 sts across cuff, place marker

With new needle, pick up 17 sts down other side of heel flap

You should now have a total of 88 sts on four needles

Rnd 1: K to within 3 sts of first marker, k2tog, k1, slip marker, k to next marker, slip marker, k1, ssk, k to end of rnd – 86 sts

Rnd 2: K

Repeat rnds 1–2 nine more times

You should now have 68 sts on your needles

● Foot

Rnds 1–40: K

Note: for a longer foot, add a few more knit rnds here.

● Toe Shaping

Rnd 1: K to within 3 sts of first marker, k2tog, k1, slip marker, k1, ssk, k to within 3 sts of next marker, k2tog, k1, slip marker, k1, ssk, k to end of rnd

Rnd 2: K

Repeat rnds 1–2 eight more times

You should now have 32 sts on your needles

Knit to first marker. Divide remaining sts on to two needles and sew up seam using Kitchener stitch

Suggestions for adaptation

If you fancy making a pair for yourself or for a female friend, chose a 4-ply yarn, and using 2.5mm double-pointed needles cast on 60 stitches. Then adapt the pattern as follows. Ribbing and cuff: work as above. Heel flap: knit 15, turn, then row 1: Sl 1, p29; row 2: Sl 1, k29; and repeat rows 1-2 fourteen more times. Heel shaping: row 1: Sl 1, p16, p2tog, p1, turn, then work following rows as above until you have 18 sts on your needle. Gusset: pick up 15 sts each side of heel flap and work as above so you have 78 sts on your needles, then work rnds 1-2 as above until you have 60 sts on your needles. Foot: knit 46 rnds. Toe shaping: work as above until you have 24 sts on your needles.

Gifts for Babies

Babies are a joy to knit for. Tiny things are always cute (especially if we're talking miniscule Mary Jane booties, see p. 152) and because you're using such small amounts of yarn, you really can go all out with the luxury stuff. Baby-pink cashmere? Delicious.

You'll need to be extra careful when choosing yarn for a baby. Their delicate skin is sensitive so make sure you go for something soft. Yarns with a tendency to shed – angora, mohair – are not a good idea; you don't want to choke the little cherub. It is a fact that babies vomit. A lot. So it's best to choose a machine-washable yarn that's strong enough to withstand frequent washing. Pure cashmere is not so good – a cashmere and cotton blend is better.

Some people think it's bad luck to knit for a baby who hasn't yet been born, but ignore that: babies grow almost as fast as you can knit so get your project started as soon as possible.

Mary Jane Booties

Booties are the perennial baby gift and you'll find a pattern for a pair in pretty much every baby knitting book you'll ever come across. Although more babies can be seen sporting socks these days, a tiny pair of booties in super-soft yarn are the cutest thing and will be preserved by mothers as family keepsakes for years to come.

Skills

Cast on: pp. 56–9
Knit: p. 62
Make one (m1): p. 69
Slip, slip, knit (ssk): p. 74
Knit two together (k2tog):
    p. 73
Cast on stitches in middle
    of a row: p. 72
Cast off: pp. 66–7

Difficulty ✳✳✳

Size
To fit newborn baby

Finished measurements
7 cm toe to heel

Materials
- Yarn: 1 x 50g Rowan Cashsoft
  4-ply in Cream (433)
- Needles: 3mm
- Stitch holders
- Two small buttons

Tension
30 sts and 60 rows = 10cm/4in square in garter stitch

Directions

Cast on 31 sts

Row 1: K

Row 2: K1, m1, k14, m1, k1, m1, k14, m1, k1 – 35 sts

Row 3: K

Row 4: K1, m1, k15, m1, k3, m1, k15, m1, k1 – 39 sts

Row 5: K

Row 6: K1, m1, k16, m1, k1, m1, k3, m1, k1, m1, k16, m1, k1 – 45 sts

Row 7: K

Row 8: K1, m1, k17, m1, k1, m1, k7, m1, k1, m1, k17, m1, k1 – 51 sts

Rows 9–19: K

Row 20: K15, (ssk) 5 times, k1, (k2tog) 5 times, k15 – 41 sts

Rows 21–3: K

● Strap – Left Bootie

Row 1: K10, cast off 9 sts, k3, cast off 9 sts, k10

Row 2: K10 (sl the other sts on to stitch holders, 3 sts on one, 10 sts on another, to free up the needle), cast on 18 sts (you'll now work across these 28 sts to make the strap)

Row 3: K

Row 4: K to last 2 sts, yo, ssk

Cast off all sts

Sl 10 sts from holder back on to needle

Rows 1–3: K

Cast off all sts

● Strap – Right Bootie

Row 1: K10, cast off 9 sts, k3, cast off 9 sts, k10

Row 2: K10, (sl the other sts on to stitch holders, 3 sts on one, 10 sts on another to free up needle), turn

Rows 3–4: K

Cast off all sts

Sl 10 sts from holder back on to needle

Row 1: K10, cast on 18 sts

Row 2: K

Row 3: K to last 2 sts, yo, ssk

Cast off all sts

● Middle Bar – Both Booties

Sl 3 sts on holder back on to needle

Work 30 rows garter st (k every row)

Cast off all sts

● Finishing

Sew up the bottom seam and along the back of the bootie. Fold over the middle bar and sew it together. Thread the strap through the middle bar and attach the button to the side

Suggestions for adaptation

Turn these Mary Jane-style booties into simple slippers by casting off all stitches on your needle after Row 23.

Simple Baby Hat

This delightful little hat was designed by the lovely girls behind my favourite blog, Pickles (see p. 188). Heidi Grønvold and Anna Enge live in Norway and, as art directors at an advertising agency, have been colleagues for years. A few years back when they both happened to be pregnant at the same time, they discovered a shared passion for knitting. They started the Pickles blog in January 2009 and in August 2009 opened their own online yarn shop.

They tell me that their inspiration for this design came from the teeny-weeny hats that are given to premature babies in Norwegian hospitals. For some reason, this little fact brings a tear to my eye.

Skills

Cast on: pp. 56–9

Knit: p. 62

Purl: p. 63

Knit in the round: pp. 78–81

Knit two together (k2tog): p. 73

Difficulty **

Size

0–6 months

Finished Measurements

31 cm circumference at widest part (unstretched)

Materials

- Yarn: 1 x 50g Rowan Extra Fine Merino DK in Cloud (881)
- Needles: 3.5mm double-pointed
- Stitch marker

Tension

23 sts and 36 rows = 10cm/4in square in stocking stitch

Directions

Cast on 70 sts. Divide sts on to three needles. Join, being careful not to twist the sts and place marker to indicate beginning of rnd

Rnds 1–5: K

Rnd 6: P

Repeat rnds 1–6 five more times

● Decrease Rounds

Rnds 1–4: K

Rnd 5: *K8, k2tog; repeat from * to end of rnd – 63 sts

Rnd 6: P

Rnds 7–10: K

Rnd 11: *K7, k2tog; repeat from * to end of rnd – 56 sts

Rnd 12: P

Rnds 13–16: K

Rnd 17: *K6, k2tog; repeat from * to end of rnd – 49 sts

Rnd 18: P

Rnds 19–22: K

Rnd 23: *K5, k2tog; repeat from * to end of rnd – 42 sts

Rnd 24: P

Rnds 25–8: K

Rnd 29: *k2tog; repeat from * to end of rnd – 21 sts

Suggestions for adaptation

This simple hat pattern can easily be knitted with an all-over stocking stitch. Just turn all the purl rows into knit rows. Easy!

Rnd 29: *k2tog; repeat from * to end of rnd – 21 sts

Rnd 30: P

Rnds 31–5: K

Cut yarn leaving a 10cm tail and thread on to a tapestry needle. Insert the tapestry needle through each of the sts, removing them from the needle as you go. Pull the yarn tight to close up the top of the hat, make a loop with the remaining yarn, pull through and weave in the yarn end to secure

'Born Under a Star' Blanket

Another creation from the Pickles team. Heidi and Anna are as obsessed with stitch patterns as I am and love dreaming up patterns to make use of a new favourite. The star stitch pattern used here inspired the girls to name this blanket 'born under a star'. Very cute.

Skills

Cast on: pp. 56–9

Knit: p. 62

Purl: p. 63

Purl three together (p3tog): p. 73

Cast off: pp. 66–7

Difficulty **

Finished Measurements

After blocking: 45cm wide, 60cm long

Materials

- Yarn: 2 x 50g Pickles Extra Fine Merino in Platina
- Needles: 6.5mm

Tension

8 sts and 24 rows = 10cm/4in square in garter stitch

Directions

Cast on 70 sts very loosely

● Garter Stitch Border

Rows 1–8: K

● Pattern Section

Row 1: K5, *MK; repeat from * to last 5 sts, k5

Row 2: K

Row 3: K6 *MK; repeat from * to last 7 sts, k7

Row 4: K

Repeat rows 1–4 until blanket measures 50cm from cast-on edge

Note: to work the MK (which is an abbreviation for 'make' and differs from pattern to pattern), purl three together but leave the stitches on the left needle, yarn over, then purl the same three together again.

● Garter Stitch Border

Rows 1–8: K

Cast off all sts loosely

The blanket will need heavy blocking to open up the lace pattern and stretch it to the correct size

Suggestions for adaptation

Really you could knit up a baby blanket in any stitch pattern you like. Check out Barbara Walker's *A Treasury of Knitting Patterns* for inspiration. Stick to the garter stitch border in the pattern above and then work away in your chosen stitch pattern for the middle section. One thing to remember when knitting blankets for babies is that they get their fingers caught in everything, so make sure your pattern doesn't create too much of an open weave where their little digits could get stuck in the holes.

Bib

A pretty knitted bib makes a nice alternative to the horrible plastic things you see most babies sporting these days (I say that like they have a choice). Cotton yarn is best here: it's machine washable and will be soft and gentle on the little one's skin.

Skills
Cast on: pp. 56–9
Knit: p. 62
Yarn over (yo): p. 71
Knit two together (k2tog): p. 73
Cast off: pp. 66–7

Difficulty *

Finished Measurements
Bib 18cm x 20cm,
strap 5cm x 25cm

Materials
- Yarn: 1 x 50g Rowan Handknit Cotton in Sugar (303)
- Needles: 4mm
- One medium-sized button

Tension
22 sts and 38 rows = 10cm/4in square in garter stitch

Directions

Cast on 38 sts

All rows: K

Work garter stitch until piece measures 20cm from cast-on edge

● Strap

Next row: Cast off 28 sts, k10

Work garter stitch until strap measures 22cm

Next row: K5, yo, k2tog, k3

Work garter stitch for nine rows

Cast off all sts

Attach button to top right corner

Suggestions for adaptation

Try knitting a bib using a different stitch pattern in the centre – moss stitch or stocking stitch would work well, as would any of the flat textured patterns like dot stitch (see iPod sock on p. 176). Or stick to a simple garter-stitch version and embroider a little initial in the corner.

Mortimer the Dog

Rebecca Danger, a knitter from Birch Bay, Washington, is the designer who created this achingly cute pattern. No boring teddy bear, Mortimer is the kind of toy who will become some little monkey's best friend. (My goddaughter Alice uses her best friend – a cuddly duck – as an excuse to leave birthday parties, by marching up to the host and announcing she has to go because 'Duckie needs to get home'.)

Rebecca has been knitting since she begged her grandma to teach her one summer holiday in California when she was twelve. Years later, Rebecca launched her online venture Danger Crafts, selling patterns for her wonderfully quirky knitted toys. She has a couple of free patterns for you to download on her blog (www.rebeccadanger.typepad.com – the 'bunny nuggets' are my favourite) or you can buy a whole heap of her other brilliant patterns from her Etsy shop: www.dangercrafts.etsy.com.

Rebecca likes to give all her creations their own personalities (honestly, what's not to love?) – here is what she says about Mortimer, the Meticulous Mutt: 'Mortimer is one organized little guy. He likes to find a place for everything and works extremely hard at keeping everything in its place. Most people call him obsessive compulsive, but Mortimer just thinks that everyone else is making excuses for not getting organized. Despite his rather obsessive personality, Mortimer makes a great friend, especially since he is very reliable and will show up early every time.' *Cute.*

The yarn you choose for this project really isn't important – you can make your dog as small or as large as you like. Just make sure you use needles two or three sizes smaller than those recommended by your yarn so that you get a nice tight-weave fabric that won't let the stuffing poke out between the stitches.

Skills

Cast on: pp. 56–9

Knit: p. 62

Knit in the round: pp. 78–81

Increase one (inc1): p. 70

Knit two together (k2tog): p. 73

Kitchener stitch: pp. 92–3

Cast off: pp. 66–7

Directions

● Body

With MC cast on 40 sts. Divide sts on to three needles. Join for working in the rnd, being careful not to twist the sts, and place marker to indicate beginning of rnd

Rnds 1–28: K

Rnd 29: (K2tog, k18) 2 times – 38 sts

Rnd 30: K

Rnd 31: (K17, k2tog) 2 times – 36 sts

Rnd 32: K

Difficulty ****

Finished Measurements
26cm head to toe,
10cm chest width

Materials
- Yarn: MC: small amount of Cascade 220 Wool in cream (8010); CC: small amount of Cascade 220 Wool in brown (8686)
- Needles: 3.75mm double-pointed
- Stitch marker
- Plastic eyes and nose
- Toy stuffing
- Sewing needle and small amounts of brown and cream cotton thread

Tension
10 sts and 24 rows = 10cm/4in square in stocking stitch

Rnd 33: (K2tog, k16) 2 times – 34 sts

Rnd 34: K

Rnd 35: (K15, k2tog) 2 times – 32 sts

Rnd 36: K

Rnd 37: (K2tog, k14) 2 times – 30 sts

Rnd 38: K

Rnd 39: (K13, k2tog) 2 times – 28 sts

Rnd 40: K

Rnd 41: (K2tog, k10, k2tog) 2 times – 24 sts

Rnd 42: (K2tog, k8, k2tog) 2 times – 20 sts

Rnd 43: (K2tog, k6, k2tog) 2 times – 16 sts

Divide sts on to two needles and sew up the seam using Kitchener stitch.

- **Ears (Make 2)**

With MC cast on 12 sts. Divide sts on to three needles. Join for working in the rnd, being careful not to twist the sts and place marker to indicate beginning of rnd

Rnds 1–2: K

Rnd 3: (Inc1, k5) 2 times – 14 sts

Rnd 4: K

Rnd 5: (K6, inc1) 2 times – 16 sts

Rnd 6: K

Rnd 7: (Inc1, k7) 2 times – 18 sts

Rnd 8: K

Rnd 9: (K8, inc1) 2 times – 20 sts

Rnds 10–15: K

Rnd 16: (K2tog, k6, k2tog) 2 times – 16 sts

Rnd 17: (K2tog, k4, k2tog) 2 times – 12 sts

Rnd 18: (K2tog, k2, k2tog) 2 times – 8 sts

Continues on next page

Divide sts evenly between two needles and sew up the seam using Kitchener stitch

Work second ear the same as the first using CC colour

● Arms (Make 2)

With MC cast on 12 sts. Divide sts on to three needles. Join for working in the rnd, being careful not to twist the sts and place marker to indicate beginning of rnd

Rnds 1–12: K

Rnd 13: *Inc1, k2; repeat from * to end of rnd – 16 sts

Rnds 14-19: K

Rnd 20: *K2tog; repeat from * to end of rnd – 8 sts

Cut yarn leaving a 10cm tail and thread on to a tapestry needle. Insert the tapestry needle through each of the sts, removing them from the needle as you go. Pull the yarn tight to close up the hand and weave the yarn end in

Work second arm the same as the first

● Legs (Make 2)

With MC cast on 14 sts. Divide sts on to three needles. Join for working in the rnd, being careful not to twist the sts and place marker to indicate beginning of rnd

Rnds 1–20: K

Rnd 21: K5, (inc1) 4 times, k5 – 18 sts

Rnd 22: K7, (inc1) 4 times, k7 – 22 sts

Rnd 23: K9, (inc1) 4 times, k9 – 26 sts

Rnd 24: K12, (inc1) 2 times, k12 – 28 sts

Rnd 25: K13, (inc1) 2 times, k13 – 30 sts

Rnds 26–9: K

Divide sts evenly between two needles and sew up the seam using Kitchener stitch

Work second leg the same as the first

● Tail

With MC cast on 9 sts. Divide sts on to three needles. Join for working in the rnd, being careful not to twist the sts and place marker to indicate beginning of rnd

Rnds 1–20: K

Rnds 21–4: With CC, k

Rnd 25: *K2tog; repeat from * to last st, k1 – 5 sts

Cut yarn leaving a 10cm tail and thread on to a tapestry needle. Insert the tapestry needle through each of the sts, removing them from the needle as you go. Pull the yarn tight to close up the seam and weave the yarn end in

● Eye spot (Make 1)

With CC cast on 4 sts. Join for working in the rnd, being careful not to twist the sts and place marker to indicate beginning of rnd

Rnd 1: *Inc1; repeat from * to end of rnd – 8 sts

Rnd 2: *Inc1; repeat from * to end of rnd – 16 sts

Rnd 3: *K1, inc1; repeat from * to end of rnd – 24 sts

Rnd 4: K

Cast off all sts purlwise

● Body spots (Make 2)

With CC cast on 6 sts. Join for working in the rnd, being careful not to twist the sts and place marker to indicate beginning of rnd

Rnd 1: *Inc1; repeat from * to end of rnd – 12 sts

Rnd 2: *Inc1; repeat from * to end of rnd – 24 sts

Rnd 3: *K1, inc1; repeat from * to end of rnd – 36 sts

Rnds 4–6: K

Cast off all sts purlwise

Work second body spot the same as the first

Continues on next page

● Finishing

Weave in yarn ends

With cotton thread and a regular sewing needle, sew the eye patch to Mortimer's face. Attach one of the plastic eyes to the centre of the patch and the second eye to the other side of his face

Attach the plastic nose

Stuff the body, tail and hands and feet (leaving the rest of the arms and legs unstuffed so that they dangle nicely)

Sew the ears, arms and tail to the body

Sew the legs to the bottom of the body on the inside (this will hide the join once Mortimer is sewn together)

Sew the two body spots on to the body (you can place these wherever you like but Rebecca likes to sew one on the side of Mortimer's body under his arm and one in the middle of his back)

Embroider a little belly button, sew the bottom seam shut and that's it: say hello to your new best friend!

Suggestions for adaptation

You can make a simpler version of Mortimer by ditching the little patches (though, really, they are so cute it would almost be criminal to do this) and knitting the tail in one colour.

gifts for the Home

Your uptight friend wouldn't be seen dead wearing any kind of 'homemade' accessory? No need to ditch her just yet – knit something for her home instead (and knitted home accessories make perfect wedding and house-warming presents too). The stunning cushion pattern on p. 164 is far more luxurious than anything you could buy at Habitat and the elegant cashmere hot-water bottle cover on p. 166 would knock Cath Kidston right off her floral pedestal.

Honeycomb Cable Cushion

This beautiful cushion cover was designed by the very talented Rose Sharp Jones. Rose has been knitting since she was a little girl and she has her own business designing and making a range of textile products. Check out the gorgeous jewellery and home accessories on her website: www.rosesharpjones.co.uk. Rose is the daughter of Susan Sharp, another of the designers who have scribbled a pattern for this book (the chic beret on p.136) and helps her mother run their yarn shop in South East London.

Honeycomb cable works so well on this cushion and is a very different (and very beautiful) alternative to the twisty ropey versions you see on fishermen's sweaters.

Skills

Cast on: pp. 56–9

Knit: p. 62

Purl: p. 63

Yarn over (yo): p. 71

Knit two together (k2tog):
  p. 73

Cable: pp. 85–6

Cast off: pp. 66–7

Mattress stitch: pp. 89–91

Difficulty ****

Finished Measurements

36cm x 36cm unstretched

Materials

- Yarn: 2 x 100g Rowan Pure
  Wool Aran in Cloud (673)
- Needles: 5mm
- Cable needle
- Three medium-sized buttons
- 35cm x 35cm cushion pad

Tension

18 sts and 30 rows = 10cm/4in square in moss stitch

Directions

Note: work cable stitches as follows:

(C4B) = slip next 2 sts onto cable needle and hold at back of work, knit next 2 sts from left hand needle, then knit the sts from the cable needle;

(C4F) = slip next 2 sts onto cable needle and hold at front of work, knit next 2 sts from left hand needle, then knit sts from cable needle.

Cast on 62sts

Rows 1–3: K

Row 4: K17, yo, k2tog, (k13, yo, k2tog) 2 times, k to end of row

Rows 5–7: K

Row 8: P

● Moss Stitch Section

Row 1: K1, *p2, k2; repeat from * to last st, k1

Row 2: P1, *k2, p2; repeat from * to last st, p1

Row 3: K1, *k2, p2; repeat from * to last st, k1

Row 4: P1, *p2, k2; repeat from * to last st, p1

Repeat rows 1–4 nineteen more times

Next row: K1, *p2, k2; repeat from * to last st, k1

Next row: P1, *k2, p2; repeat from * to last st, p1

Next row: P

Next row: K

Cable Section

Row 1: K2, *inc1, k2; repeat from * to end of row – 82 sts

Row 2: P

Row 3: K1, *C4B, C4F; repeat from * to last st, k1

Row 4: P

Row 5: K

Row 6: P

Row 7: K1, *C4F, C4B; repeat from * to last st, k1

Row 8: P

Repeat rows 1–8 of cable pattern five more times but instead of working the increases on row 1, work knit sts across the row

Next row: P2, *p2tog, p2; repeat from * to end of row – 62 sts

Next row: K

Moss Stitch Section

Row 1: K1, *p2, k2; repeat from * to last st, k1

Row 2: P1, *k2, p2; repeat from * to last st, p1

Row 3: K1, *k2, p2; repeat from * to last st, k1

Row 4: P1, *p2, k2; repeat from * to last st, p1

Repeat rows 1-4 sixteen more times

Cast off all sts

Finishing

The cable section will be narrower than the double moss stitch sections but don't worry because when you sew up the seams, the cable section will stretch to be the same width.

Fold bottom of cushion up (right sides out) so that cast-off edge is approximately 14cm from bottom fold. Fold top of cushion down so that cast-on edge is approximately 25cm from top fold (there should be approximately 3.5cm of overlap). Pin in place and sew up side seams using mattress stitch. Attach buttons to correspond with buttonholes

Suggestions for adaptation

For a simpler version of this beautiful cushion, knit the whole thing in moss stitch. Cast on 62 sts and knit the first six rows as above. Start knitting the first moss stitch section as above but instead of knitting just twenty repeats of the moss stitch pattern, keep going until the piece measures 77cm from cast-on edge. Cast off and finish as above.

Hot-Water Bottle Cover

Elly Fales, who writes the seriously aspirational blog Green Olives Design (see p. 187), designed this luxury hot-water bottle cover. Elly's mother taught her to knit when she was twelve using a pair of chopsticks from the silverware drawer and she's been hooked ever since. She recently moved from the busy city to a green house on the edge of a small town in Montana. Now she finds more time to enjoy the things she loves: sewing, knitting, cooking and sticking her camera in the faces of her husband, daughter and Karelian bear dog. See for yourself on her Flickr page: www.flickr.com/photos/olivgron, but be warned – will most likely induce severe lifestyle envy.

Skills

Cast on: pp. 56–9

Knit: p. 62

Knit in the round: pp. 78–81

Make one (m1): p. 69

Knit two together (k2tog): p. 73

Slip, slip, knit (ssk): p. 74

Cast off: pp. 66–7

Kitchener stitch: pp. 92–3

Difficulty **

Finished Measurements

20cm wide, 42cm long

Materials

- Yarn: 3 x 50g Rowan Cashsoft Aran in Oat (001)
- Needles: 4.5mm double-pointed
- Stitch markers

Tension

22 sts and 30 rows = 10cm/4in square in stocking stitch

Directions

● Neck

Cast on 44 sts. Divide sts on to three needles. Join, being careful not to twist the sts and place marker to indicate beginning of rnd

Rnds 1–44: K2, p2 to end of rnd

● Increase Rounds

Rnd 1: *K4, m1; repeat from * to end of rnd – 55 sts

Rnd 2: *K5, m1; repeat from * to end of rnd – 66 sts

Rnd 3: *K6, m1; repeat from * to end of rnd – 77 sts

● Body

Continue to knit all rnds until body measures 25cm

● Decrease Rounds

Next rnd (removing marker): K35, ssk, k1, place marker, k2tog, k34, ssk, k1, place marker, k2tog – 73 sts

Next rnd: K to within 3 sts of first marker, ssk, k1, slip marker, k2tog, k to within 3 sts of second marker, ssk, k1, slip marker, k2tog – 69 sts

Next rnd: K to within 3 sts of first marker, ssk, k1, slip marker, k2tog, k to within 3 sts of second marker, ssk, k1, slip marker, k2tog – 65 sts

Next rnd: K to within 3 sts of first marker, ssk, k1, slip marker, k2tog, k to within 3 sts of second marker, ssk, k1, slip marker, k2tog – 61 sts

Next rnd: K to within 3 sts of first marker, ssk, k1, slip marker, k2tog, k to within 3 sts of second marker, ssk, k1, slip marker k3tog – 56 sts (pay attention here: you're making a k3tog instead of a k2tog at the end)

Divide remaining sts on to two needles and sew up seam using Kitchener stitch

● Pocket

Cast on 30 sts using straight needles (or two of your DPNs)

Row 1: P2, k to last 2 sts, p2

Row 2: K2, p to last 2 sts, k2

Row 3: K

Row 4: P

Repeat rows 1–4 until piece measures 14cm

Cast off all sts

Sew pocket to cover

Suggestions for adaptation

For a more personalized version of this hot-water bottle cover, ditch the pocket and work the initial of the recipient in intarsia on the front (see p. 82 for how).

Tea Cosy

The tea cosy was invented by the ever-so-fanciful Victorians. This sophisticated version, designed by Ruth Bridgman, couldn't be further from the kind you'd find in your grandmother's cupboard. After graduating from her fashion textile design degree in 2004, Ruth set up her own boutique, Ruth Cross (the name is in homage to her grandmother), where she sells her beautiful knitted clothes, jewellery and home accessories. This is hand-knitted luxury at its very best and Ruth's designs are much in demand – I'm talking Elle Decoration *here but bizarrely, that creepy girl from* Twilight *wears a pair of Ruth's mittens in the film. You can buy Ruth's creations from various stockists around the country, on her website (www.ruthcross.com) or in person at her boutique in Salisbury.*

Skills

Cast on: pp. 56–9

Knit: p. 62

Purl: p. 63

Yarn over (yo): p. 71

Cast on in middle of row: p. 72

Cast off: pp. 66–7

Difficulty ✳✳✳

Finished Measurements

Cast-on edge (excluding button loop) 45cm

Materials

- Yarn: 1 x 100g Cascade Baby Alpaca Chunky in Mimosa (552)
- Needles: 6mm
- One medium-sized button

Tension

6 sts and 22 rows = 10cm/4in square in pattern stitch

Directions

Cast on 66 sts

Rows 1–2: P

Row 3: Cast on 8sts, cast off 8 sts, k3, (yo, k4) 4 times, k28, (k4, yo) 4 times, k2 – 74 sts

Row 4: P1, *k2, p2; repeat from * to last st, p1

Row 5: *K2, p2; repeat from * to last 2 sts, k2

Repeat rows 4–5 three more times

Row 12: P1, (k2, p2) 8 times, k2, cast off 4 sts, p2 (one of these p sts will already be worked by casting off), (k2, p2) 8 times, p1 – you should have 35 sts either side of the cast-off sts

Using two separate strands of yarn, continue working both halves

Row 13: (K2, p2) 8 times, k2, p1, switch yarn, p1, (k2, p2) 8 times, k2

Row 14: P1, (k2, p2) 8 times, k2, switch yarn, p2, (k2, p2) 8 times, p1

Repeat rows 13–14 five more times

Row 25: Repeat row 13

Next row work across, joining both halves together

Row 26: P1, *k2, p2; repeat from * to last st, p1 – 70 sts

Row 27: *K2, p2; repeat from * to last 2 sts, k2

Repeat rows 26–7 two more times

Row 32: P1, *k2tog, p2tog; repeat from * to last st, p1 – 36 sts

Row 33: *K2tog; repeat from * to end of row – 18 sts

Row 34: *P2tog; repeat from * to end or row – 9 sts

Cut yarn leaving a 20cm tail and thread onto a tapestry needle. Insert the tapestry needle through each of the sts, starting from the furthest st (so that you make a loop), removing them from the needle as you go. Pull the yarn to close up the top of the cosy leaving a hole that measures 2cm across

● Finishing

Making sure the hole doesn't close, start sewing up the seam along the side of the cosy and stop when you get to the point where the top of your teapot handle will be (you'll want to get the teapot out to find out how far to sew up the seam). Turn the button loop back on itself and sew up the end. Attach button to correspond with button loop

Suggestions for adaptation

Give this classic tea cosy a more retro look and knit it up in stripes. Just pick your second colour and alternate every two or three rows.

Cafetière Cosy

The modern equivalent of the tea cosy. These days, most of us use our cafetières more than our teapots so knit up one of these and pair it with a tea cosy (p. 168) for the perfect gift for a friend who falls at the feet of vintage chic.

Skills
Cast on: pp. 56–9

Knit: p. 62

Purl: p. 63

Slip stitch (sl 1): p. 74

Purl two together (p2tog): p. 73

Cast off: pp. 66–7

Difficulty *

Finished Measurements
25cm wide, 12cm long

Materials
- Yarn: 1 x 100g Cascade Baby Alpaca Chunky in Ecru (565)
- Needles: 6mm
- Three small buttons

Tension
22 sts and 22 rows = 10cm/4in square in twisted purl stitch

Directions

Cast on 50 sts

Row 1: Sl 1, k to end of row

Row 2: *P2tog but leave sts on left needle, purl the first st again then slip both sts from needle together; repeat from * to end of row

Row 3: Sl 1, k to end of row

Row 4: P1, *p2tog but leave sts on left needle, purl the first st again then slip both sts from needle together; repeat from * to last st, p1

Repeat rows 1–4 until piece measures 11.5cm from cast-on edge

Cast off all sts

• Finishing

Cut three pieces of yarn 25cm in length and plait together to make a cord. Make a loop with the plaited cord and poke it up from the back of the work to the front at the top right hand corner. Making sure the loop doesn't close up, secure the cord ends at the back of the work. Make two more plaited cords and attach them as above, one at the bottom right hand corner and one in the middle. Attach the three buttons to the left selvedge edge to correspond with button loops

Suggestions for adaptation

Easy. Pick your stitch pattern, make a tension swatch (see p. 100-101) and work out how many stitches you need to cast on to get a width of 25cm. Then just work the pattern until piece measures 11.5cm from cast-on edge and finish as above.

Novelty Gifts

For when you don't have the time or energy to spend hours on your gifts. All the patterns in this section are super easy and super quick and can be customized with stitch patterns, stripes or fancy yarns to make them ideal last-minute presents.

Covered Bangles

Inspired by a picture I saw in Vogue a while back of something similar (but much more expensive), these pretty knitted bangles look impressive but are so easy to make. In fact, this is officially the easiest (and quickest) pattern in the whole book. All you have to do is make a rectangular swatch and sew up the seams around the bangle. It honestly could not be more straightforward.

Skills

Cast on: pp. 56–9
Knit: p. 62
Purl: p. 63
Cabling: pp. 85–6
Cast off: pp. 66–7
Backstitch: pp. 88–9

Difficulty *

Materials

- Yarn: for Cable bangle, 1 x 100g Malabrigo Worsted in Pigeon; for double moss stitch bangle, 1 x 50g Rowan Extra Fine Merino DK in Graphite (990); for fleck stitch bangle, 1 x 100g ball of Skein Queen Plushness in lemon chiffon
- Needles: for Cable bangle, 4.5mm; for double moss stitch bangle, 3.5mm; for fleck stitch bangle: 3mm
- Cable needle
- Bangle

Directions

Wrap a tape measure around the bangle (width) and along the outer circumference (length) and take a note of the two measurements. Knit up a tension swatch (see pp. 100–101 for how) in your chosen stitch pattern (either the cable stitch, double moss stitch or fleck stitch below, or another pattern of your own choosing) to work out how many stitches you'll need to cast on to yield a piece of fabric the same width as your bangle measurement. Then . . .

● Cable Bangle

Cast on 16 sts (or number of sts required to yield the correct size for your bangle)

Row 1: P5, k6, p5

Row 2: K5, p6, k5

Row 3: P5, C6F, p5

Row 4: K5, p6, k5

Row 5: P5, k6, p5

Row 6: K5, p6, k5

Repeat rows 1–6 until piece measures the same length as your bangle (the outer circumference measurement)

Cast off all sts

● Double Moss Stitch Bangle

Cast on 26 sts (or number of sts required to yield the correct size for your bangle – must be a multiple of 4 sts plus 2)

Rows 1–2: K2, *p2, k2; repeat from * to end of row

Rows 3–4: P2, *k2, p2; repeat from * to end of row

Repeat rows 1–4 until piece measures the same length as your
   bangle (the outer circumference measurement)

Cast off all sts

● Fleck Stitch Bangle

Cast on 15 sts (or number of sts required to yield the correct size for
   your bangle – must be a multiple of 2 sts plus 1)

Row 1: K

Row 2: P

Row 3: K1, *p1, k1; repeat from * to end of row

Row 4: P

Repeat rows 1–4 until piece measures the same length as your
   bangle (the outer circumference measurement)

Cast off all sts

● Finishing

Wrong sides facing, line up cast-on edge with cast-off edge and sew
   up seam using backstitch. Turn the right way around and slip over
   your bangle. Fold over and sew up seam along the circumference
   of your bangle. Adjust so that seam sits inside the bangle in the
   centre and out of sight

Suggestions for adaptation

See the fancy-pants stitches on pp. 105–109 or refer to the Bible
(otherwise known as Barbara Walker's *A Treasury of Knitting
Patterns*) for inspiration. If your basic bangle is a handsome thing
that ought not to be hidden completely, pick an open-weave stitch
to show it off.

Lacy Bracelets

Another pretty pattern from textiles designer Rose Sharp Jones. Rose has some gorgeous crochet bracelets on her website and has designed this equally lovely knitted version especially for you. This bracelet is easy and quick to knit, which makes it a great last-minute gift for your girly friends and family.

Skills

Cast on: pp. 56–9

Knit: p. 62

Purl: p. 63

Knit two together (k2tog): p. 73

Yarn over (yo): p. 71

Cast off: pp. 66–7

Difficulty **

Finished Measurements

17cm long, 7cm wide

Materials

- Yarn: 1 x 50g Artesano 4-ply Alpaca in Bonbon (SFN41)
- Needles: 2.75mm
- Three small buttons

Tension

30 sts and 30 rows = 10cm/4in square in garter stitch

Directions

Cast on 58 sts

Row 1: K2, p to last 2 sts, k2

Rows 2–3: K

Row 4: Repeat row 1

Row 5: K2tog, yo, (k2tog) 3 times, (yo, k1) 6 times, (k2tog) 6 times, (yo, k1) 6 times, (k2tog) 6 times, (yo, k1) 6 times, (k2tog) 3 times, k2

Rows 6–7: K

Row 8: Repeat row 1

Row 9: K2, (k2tog) 3 times, (yo, k1) 6 times, (k2tog) 6 times, (yo, k1) 6 times, (k2tog) 6 times, (yo, k1) 6 times, (k2tog) 3 times, k2

Rows 10–11: K

Row 12: Repeat row 1

Row 13: Repeat row 9

Rows 14–15: K

Row 16: Repeat row 1

Row 17: Repeat row 5

Rows 18–19: K

Row 20: Repeat row 1

Row 21: Repeat row 9

Rows 22–3: K

Row 24: Repeat row 1

Row 25: Repeat row 9

Rows 26–7: K

Row 28: Repeat row 1

Row 29: Repeat row 5

Row 30: K

Row 31: P

Cast off all sts tightly. Sew buttons on to correspond with buttonholes

Suggestions for adaptation

This bracelet could be knitted using any 4-ply yarn you like. Try a mohair blend for a fuzzy effect or a plain cotton for something a little more structured.

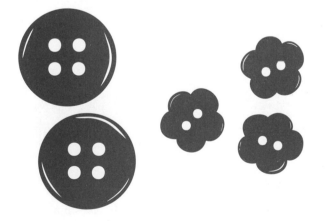

iPod Sock

I don't know many people who don't own an iPod, but I know plenty who have a very scratched one. An iPod sock (or an iPhone sock for that matter) is a fantastic last-minute gift for boyfriends, girlfriends, cool dads and teenaged relations.

Skills

Cast on: pp. 56–9
Knit: p. 62
Purl: p. 63
Slip stitch (sl 1): p. 74
Cast off: pp. 66–7
Mattress stitch: pp. 89–91

Difficulty *

Sizes
iPod (iPhone)

Finished Measurements
iPod sock: 6cm wide,
10.5cm long
iPhone sock: 6cm wide,
13cm long

Materials
- Yarn: 1 x 50g Rowan Extra Fine Merino DK in Powder (883) and Graphite (990)
- Needles: 3.5mm

Tension
26 sts and 38 rows = 10cm/4in square in dot stitch
28 sts and 38 rows = 10cm/4in square in slip rib stitch

Directions

● Dot Stitch Sock

Cast on 19 sts

Row 1: K1, *p1, k3; repeat from * to last 2 sts, p1, k1

Row 2: P

Row 3: *K3, p1; repeat from * to last 3 sts, k3

Row 4: P

Repeat rows 1–4 until piece measures 22cm (25cm for an iPhone) from cast-on edge

Cast off all sts

Sew up side seams

● Slip Rib Stitch Sock

Cast on 19 sts

Row 1: K1, *sl 1, k1; repeat from * to end of row

Row 2: P

Repeat rows 1–2 until piece measures 22cm (25cm for an iPhone) from cast-on edge

Cast off all sts

Sew up side seams

Note: slip stitches purlwise (as you always would when slipping on their own) but keep the yarn at the back as if you were going to knit.

Suggestions for adaptation

Experiment with different stitch patterns or go for a simpler version with garter stitch, stocking stitch or a simple rib. See pp. 64–5.

Laptop Case

Another gift for the technology bod in your life. Shop-bought laptop cases are nasty-looking things and this one here is both functional and pretty. It's a winner.

Skills
Cast on: pp. 56–9
Knit: p. 62
Purl: p. 63
Yarn over (yo): p. 71
Knit two together (k2tog):
    p. 73
Cast off: pp. 66–7
Backstitch: pp. 88–91

Difficulty *

Finished Measurements
24cm wide, 35cm long
(unstretched)

Materials
- Yarn: 2 x 100g Rowan Big
  Wool in Madras (050)
- Needles: 10mm
- Two large buttons

Tension
10 sts and 14 rows = 10cm/4in
square in stocking stitch

Directions

Cast on 25 sts

Row 1: K

Row 2: P

Repeat rows 1–2 until piece measures 66cm from cast-on edge

● Garter Stitch Band

Rows 1–21: K

Row 22: K5, yo, k2tog, k11, k2tog, yo, k5

Rows 23–8: K

Cast off all sts

● Finishing

Fold piece over so that cast-on edge lines up with the first row of the garter stitch band. Sew up side seams (backstitch is ideal here to create a sturdy seam). Attach buttons to front to correspond with buttonholes

Suggestions for adaptation

This pattern was specifically designed for a MacBook but you could easily adapt for other laptops. Measure the width of your laptop and experiment with the number of cast-on stitches until you yield a piece of fabric that is the width of the laptop plus 4cm. Then simply follow the pattern above, working in stocking stitch until your piece measures the same length as your laptop, and then knit the garter stitch band as above.

Where to Find More Patterns

The patterns in this book are a great place to begin but once you've worked your way through them (and you will), you'll need to know where else to look for ideas.

Books

There are hundreds of knitting books in print these days but with all the free patterns available on the internet, only a few of them are really worth investing in.

If you're up for trying some slightly more off-the-wall projects, look no further than Rachael Matthew's sparkly book *Knitorama* (2005, and its crochet companion, *Hookorama*, 2006). This really fun book will show you how to make things you never knew you needed, from knitted cakes and sandwiches to bras and knickers.

Many of the major yarn companies like Rowan and Debbie Bliss publish their own books and magazines. But fashion changes so quickly that I tend to find only one or two of the designs in each book are things I really want to make. Designs for baby clothes, however, are timeless and books with patterns exclusively for little chidlers can be well worth shelling out for. My two particular favourites are: *Baby Knits for Beginners* (2003) by Debbie Bliss and *Simple Knits for Cherished Babies* (2001) by Erika Knight – both have patterns for some truly beautiful baby booties, hats, blankets and clothes with clear and simple instructions to follow.

For something a little more frivolous and fun, check out *100 Flowers to Knit and Crochet* (2009) by Lesley Stanfield, which shows you how to make some lovely little flowers to embellish your projects or make knitted jewellery (really, not as gross and 'craft fair' as you might think).

Books

- *Knitorama* by Rachael Matthews
- *Baby Knits for Beginners* by Debbie Bliss
- *Simple Knits for Cherished Babies* by Erika Knight
- *100 Flowers to Knit and Crochet* by Leslie Stanfield
- *Knitting Without Tears* by Elizabeth Zimmermann
- *A Treasury of Knitting Patterns* by Barbara Walker
- *A Pictoral Guide to Modern Home Knitting*

Knitting Without Tears (1971) by Elizabeth Zimmermann is a must-read. The Martha Stewart of the knitting world, British-born Elizabeth Zimmermann, known affectionately to knitters as EZ, is widely hailed as a knitting hero. Through her books and her 1970s show on American television Elizabeth revolutionized knitting for the masses and inspired knitters the world over with her opinionated outlook and witty musings (and the fact that she could knit riding on the back of her husband's motorbike). Her advice in this book is not only useful, it's also pretty damn funny. Who knew knitting could be so amusing? Of anti-knitters, Zimmermann says: 'If you hate to knit, why, bless you, don't; follow your secret heart and take up something else.' Quite.

My Desert Island knitting book (what a strange idea) would have to be Barbara Walker's *A Treasury of Knitting Patterns* (1968). The title of this amazing book is a little misleading because it doesn't include any actual patterns but rather pages and pages of stitches. Stitch patterns are a great way to pretty up an otherwise boring bit of knitting – see pp. 105–109 for my favourite stitch patterns and how to make them. Walker's books (there are four in this particular series) aren't that easy to get hold of in the UK so you'll have to buy from US Amazon (www.amazon.com) or hope that your local yarn shop can sort you out.

I have a bit of a thing for vintage knitting books, not so much for the patterns – the desire to knit myself a bathing suit ain't exactly burning – as for the clear instructions for every knitting technique you could ever need to know. My favourite is *The Pictorial Guide to Modern Home Knitting* from 1939. It's so comprehensive I use it as my knitting encyclopaedia. It also has some pretty fabulous old-school patterns that one day I might be brave enough to try. You can find vintage knitting books in junkshops, charity shops and on eBay.

Online

Although I have a rather large (and growing) collection of knitting books, I find the majority of my patterns online. You could type 'tea cosy knitting pattern' into Google and I'm sure eventually you'd find something you'd like to make, but there are a few websites that have made the whole process of finding a pattern a hell of a lot easier.

My Desert Island knitting book would have to be Barbara Walker's A Treasury of Knitting Patterns (1968).

Ravelry (www.ravelry.com) is like Facebook for knitters and really is the most brilliant thing. Once you've set up a free account, you can keep track of the yarn and needles in your stash, log your works in progress (WIPs if you must call them that), upload pictures of your finished projects, post your own patterns, search for other people's patterns and communicate with knitters from all over the world. It's the perfect place to look for patterns – type 'socks' into the search field and a ton of designs will ping right back at you, most of them free to download. You can then 'favourite' the patterns you especially like so you can easily find them again. Like all great inventions, I can't remember what life was like before it. I salute Jessica and Casey Forbes, the genius husband-and-wife duo who came up with the idea.

Another great resource is Knitty (www.knitty.com), a free web-only Canadian magazine, published four times a year. Each issue is crammed with articles, technical advice and free patterns, and previous issues are all available on the site. Sign up for their newsletter to be notified when it comes online.

Knitting Pattern Central (www.knittingpatterncentral.com) is a directory of links to thousands of free knitting patterns. They also have a tutorials directory. It's kind of a redundant resource now that we have the almighty Ravelry and it can be a bore having to click through all the duds to find a goodie, but there are some gems to be found via this site that won't be on Ravelry so do have a look.

Bloggers are incredibly generous with their patterns and are usually happy to answer questions if you get stuck on a particular instruction. There are more inspiring, sparkling, beautiful and useful knitting blogs floating around in the internet ether than I could ever list here so if you only look at one, make sure it's Purl Bee (www.purlbee.com). This lively and attractive blog is written by the wonderful women who work at Purl Soho, a knitter's pilgrimage site in New York, and is packed full of free patterns, technical tutorials and general knitty chitchat. There are also charming (and free) crochet, embroidery and patchwork patterns for you to try. See pp. 187–8 for a further list of inspiring blogs to visit.

Bloggers are incredibly generous with their patterns and are usually happy to answer questions if you get stuck

Presenting Your Presents

If you've spent hours slaving over your needles to knit something gorgeous for a friend, you don't want to spoil the effect by then wrapping your gift in some crappy paper. Presentation is key. Here are some ideas for prettying up your presents:

- If you don't want to spend lots of money on wrapping paper, pick up some cheap brown packing paper from the post office. It looks lovely tied up with some leftover yarn (I have a huge stash of my grandmother's mohair I use especially for this purpose). Coloured tissue paper that matches your knitted gift will work just as well.

- Save old gift boxes or posh chocolate boxes and cover them in pretty paper. Stuff them with tissue paper and lay your lovingly knitted gift on top.

- If you're a proficient sewer (and actually, even if you aren't), you could knock up some super-simple cotton drawstring bags to hold your gift. All you need to do is cut out a long rectangle shape, fold it in half, sew up the seams along the side stopping 2cm before the top, fold the top 1cm over on each side and stitch the seams up leaving enough space for a drawstring. Turn the whole thing inside out, thread some chunky yarn through the top seams to make a drawstring and tie a knot in one end. Simple.

- Or, of course, you could knit a simple bag. Make a long stocking-stitch rectangle with a buttonhole at one end (see p. 87 for how). With wrong sides facing, fold the rectangle in half leaving a gap of 3–4cm to fold the top over. Sew up the sides with mattress stitch (see p. 89) and attach a button to the front.

SHARE THE LOVE

(Or what to do with your new obsession)

Knitting Groups

Curling up on the sofa on a Friday evening with your knitting and a good movie may well be the perfect way to relax after a long week at work. But knitting is so much more than just a good excuse to watch crap telly. Elizabeth Zimmermann very aptly described knitting as 'solace, inspiration, adventure', and getting out there and sharing that adventure with others – whether at a group, online or at a special knitting event – is really what it's all about.

If you're new to knitting and have caught the bug in a big way, joining a knitting group (or starting your own) is the perfect way to share the love with others and seek the advice of experts to help you hone your skills.

I love knitting with my friends. Every Friday lunchtime in my office, a small group of us find an empty meeting room, sit down together and knit. We eat our crappy canteen sandwiches, we gossip and we help each other with our knitting – whether that's showing someone how to cast on for the first (or fifth) time or working out what the hell a certain instruction in a pattern means. Our little 'crafternoon' sessions create the perfect environment for us all to learn: there's no showing off about who can turn the tidiest heel and we all feel at ease to make mistakes and ask for help. We relax, we have fun and we feel energized to tackle the last few hours of the working week.

If you're new to knitting and have caught the bug in a big way, joining a knitting group (or starting your own) is the perfect way to share the love with others and seek the advice of experts to help you hone your skills. And let's be clear here: knitting groups aren't just for genteel ladies of a certain age who hop from choir practice to book group in a desperate bid to make the most of their retirement: knitting groups are cool.

Join a Group

Join the knit revolution and seek out others to get down and knit with. The chances are that a number of knitting groups will already be up and running in your area and all you have to do is find one and rock up (preferably with cakes).

If you're in London, your first port of call should be the Stitch and Bitch London group. This massive knitting group (4,000 members and counting) meet in various venues around London once a week on a weeknight from 6 p.m. The five lovely ladies who run the group are always on hand to help you out with your knitting and generally inspire you with their 'Stitchette' charm. Visit their website for details of upcoming meetings: www.stitchandbitchlondon.co.uk.

If you're looking for something a little more intimate or you don't happen to live in Blighty, check out www.stitchnbitch.org or www.knitchicks.co.uk to find a group near you.

Start Your Own

Can't find a knitting group in your area? Don't want to hang out with strangers? No worries, it's easy to start your own group. All you need to do is find some people who already knit or would like to learn (and these days, that's pretty much everyone). If, for some unfathomable reason, your friends are too boring to join you, post a message on the Ravelry forum or on the knitting groups page of the Angel Yarns forum (www.knittingforums.co.uk) and you'll soon find some like-minded sorts living in your area who are up for hooking up.

Some things to remember if you're starting your own knitting group:

- Don't be tempted to hold your meetings at home unless it's a knitting group of close friends.
- Choose a location with enough room for everyone to sit down and enough light to see what they hell they are knitting. Dark, standing-room-only bar = bad. Open, airy café with lots of seating = good.

Guerrilla Knitting

A book about the knit would not be complete without mentioning the recent craze for guerrilla knitting (i.e., graffiti using yarn instead of paint). Knitta Please, an underground art collective who hail from Houston, Texas, were one of the first guerrilla-knitting crews to 'yarn bomb' their local area. Back in 2005, the subversive group of knitters were frustrated with all the blankets and sweaters they never completed and decided to put their unfinished projects to use by slipping them on road signs and door handles around the city. Since 2005, the tag team of knitters (whose motto is 'Warming the world, one car antenna at a time') have been yarnbombing all over the world, and in some pretty daring places – the Great Wall of China and Brooklyn Bridge, among others. Contrary to what you might think, knitted graffiti isn't a particularly political pursuit (which is a good thing as far as I'm concerned; we're way past the idea that knitting in itself   >

can make any kind of interesting point), it's more about trying to make ugly public spaces more cuddly and prompting a few smiles in the process. Check out Knitta's website for details of their latest exploits: www.knittaplease.com.

Inspired by the work of Knitta Please, a group of UK knitters formed their own knitted graffiti entity, Knit the City, in early 2009. Since then they have covered the ugly barriers in Covent Garden, London, with knitted cosies, attached tiny knitted sculptures to the six London churches that feature in the old English nursery rhyme 'Oranges and Lemons', created a giant web full of knitted creatures inside a dingy tunnel and covered a phonebox in Parliament Square with its own fully functioning cosy. Oh, the japes. If you live in London and happen upon an unusually fuzzy-looking lamppost or a tiny knitted flower hidden in a bush, chances are it'll be the work of KTC. Take a look at their website for the full stories behind Knit the City's weird and wonderful projects: www.knitthecity.com.

- Make sure the venue is easily accessible, in the centre of town or near public transport.
- Get the email addresses of everyone in the group and set up a mailing list to keep people informed about upcoming meeting details.
- Keep meetings to the same day every week or month.
- Don't come over all matron-like and start trying to force people to attend every session; instead go for a 'drop-in' approach.

Knitting Events

There are a couple of fantastic weekend events in the UK that will satisfy the more dedicated knitter. The I Knit Weekender is a particularly good one. Organized by the guys (and they really are guys – who'd have thunk it) who run the London shop I Knit, it's a fun-packed weekend of workshops, talks and shopping. Check their website for details of upcoming events: www.iknit.org.uk.

The Knitting and Stitching Show (www.twistedthread.com) travels around the country in the winter months. It's massive and can be a little overwhelming if you're not used to these kinds of shows. There's something of the absurd about the sheer volume of Doreens and Maureens shuffling around Ally Pally (the closest thing to Nanageddon you'll ever see), but it's well worth a visit if you skip the 'quilts from around the world' exhibitions and head straight for the workshops and the shopping. All the major yarn companies are represented at the show as well as a load of independent sellers, so it's a great place to stock up on yarn, needles, books and other knitting bits you never knew you needed.

The Joys of Knitting Blogs

Largely responsible for the widespread renaissance of the craft, the internet is an essential resource for knitters. Sites like Ravelry and Knitty and those of all the bloggers who are sharing their latest knitting projects with hundreds of dedicated followers have allowed knitters the world over to join forces and spread the love.

If you're new to knitting, and even if you're not, reading knitting blogs can be a great way to keep you motivated, give you ideas for new patterns and yarns to try and generally just inspire the hell out of you. They also allow you to feel connected to other knitters all around the world who share the same passion for the craft that you do. Here are some of my favourites:

If you're new to knitting, and even if you're not, reading knitting blogs can be a great way to keep you motivated, give you ideas for new patterns and yarns to try and generally just inspire the hell out of you.

Blogs for Inspriration

- Brooklyn Tweed (www.brooklyntweed.blogspot.com): a knitting blog written by a man – holy knit! Jared's popular and very lively blog will introduce you to his classic and sophisticated designs.

- Green Olives Design (www.greenolivesdesign.blogspot.com): the blog of Elly Fales, who designed the elegant hot-water bottle cover in this book (see p. 166). She is a designer and mother from Montana, makes beautiful clothes as well as knits and has an eye for all things vintage.

- Juju Loves Polkadots (www.jujulovespolkadots.typepad.com): Juju's blog tracks her love of everything crafty from beading, knitting, crochet and even rag rug making. Her eye for colour brings me a great deal of joy.

- Little Cotton Rabbits (www.littlecottonrabbits.typepad.co.uk): Julie makes tiny knitted animals (her particular thing is rabbits) and this is her inspirational blog about knitting and living with a severely autistic son.

- Pickles (www.pickles.no): a blog which incorporates Heidi and Anna's love of knitting, crochet, sewing and cupcakes. They design the cutest knitting patterns (see pp. 154 and 156), most of which are available for free on their blog, and share their yummy-looking cupcake recipes too. Oh, the joy!

- Purl Bee (www.purlbee.com): the blog of my favourite shop in the world, Purl Soho in New York. Not just about knitting but quilting, sewing and crochet too, the blog has free patterns and some excellent technique tutorials.

- Spud and Chloe (www.spudandchloe.com/blog): Spud and Chloe make lovely yarns and this is their blog, with details of their latest yarns and free patterns.

- Yarn Harlot (www.yarnharlot.ca/blog): Canadian super-knitter Stephanie McPhee is the author of a number of lively books about knitting and her witty blog was one of the first (and best) of its kind.

- Yarnstorm (www.yarnstorm.blogs.com): Jane Brocket's aspirational blog is probably the most popular knitting blog in the UK. She has a particular penchant for knitting socks (see p. 138) and writes about everything from quilting, baking, gardening, books, films and the joys of domestic life. Since 2007, Jane has also been a published author – her beautiful books about the gentle art of domesticity, quilting, cooking and knitting are worth checking out too.

- Ysolda (www.ysolda.com/wordpress): Scottish designer Ysolda Teague is an inspiration to many and it seems that pretty much everyone on Ravelry is busy knitting one of her beautiful designs, some of which are available for free on her blog.

Start Your Own Blog

Why not join the likes of the above and start your own blog? It's a fantastic way to keep a record of your knitting projects, seek advice and encouragement from other knitters and test-run your pattern ideas.

Setting up a blog is easy and free and you don't have to be a computer whiz or know anything about HTML programming to get going. All you have to do is choose a blog host – Blogger is good and free to use (www.blogger.com), as is Wordpress (www.wordpress.org) – pick a snappy name and start typing away. Posterous (http://posterous.com) is the one to go for it you're a real technophobe – you don't even have to set up an account; just email them your text and any images you want to use and they'll create the blog post for you.

Some things to remember if you're starting your own blog:

- It's all about the pictures. May I just repeat, it's *all* about the pictures. Reading about what you're knitting is no fun if the reader can't actually see the damn thing.

- Don't get too text heavy: keep your posts short and simple and don't waffle. Again, let the pictures do most of the talking.

- Keep it personal. People like to feel connected to the authors of the blogs they read. My favourite blogs have me hooked because of the personalities of the people who write them, not just because of what they are knitting.

- Don't just write about knitting. Writing about the things you like and the things that inspire or detract you from your knitting will keep your readers interested.

- Include lots of links. People who read blogs are usually all-round internet bods and like to be alerted to other blogs, sites and shops they might like because you like them too.

Making Money

If you find yourself so addicted to knitting and purling that you're churning out more scarves than you can give away, you could consider selling your knitted creations to the poor souls who aren't fortunate enough to possess the skills themselves. Etsy (www.etsy.com) is the best place to do this.

Setting up your own Etsy shop is easy and the costs are very reasonable: you pay 20 cents per item to list it in your shop for four months and then once your item sells, you make an offering to the Etsy gods to the tune of 3.5 per cent. So if your hand-knitted scarf, hat or whatever it is you're trying to flog doesn't sell within four months, you'll only be down 20 cents. You can't really afford not to do it.

Further down the line, you may even find you have a knack for designing your own patterns. It's nice to give patterns away for free on a blog but if you're business-minded (or a bit tight), you could consider selling them on Etsy or Ravelry.

Knitting for Charity

Sure, I lug all my old clothes down to Oxfam every few months and will happily drop my spare change into a collection tin at the newsagents, but I really begrudge being cajoled into being charitable.

I can't stand those crazed out-of-work actors lurking on London street corners who try to force you into signing away a portion of your salary to their charity. Their passive-aggressive approach doesn't make me feel charitable, especially when the same grinning idiot pounces three times when I venture out on my lunch break. And I'm sick of getting those emails with a link to some donation website asking me to sponsor someone I vaguely know to run a couple of miles. It's such a faceless (and lazy) way to squeeze people for cash – what happened to bringing round a form and a collection tin? Honestly, and I know I'm missing the point here slightly, if you can't even be bothered to come and talk to me or pick up the phone and tell me what the cause means to you, why should I give up a wodge of my hard-earned cash in honour of you shuffling a few miles?

But just because I don't want to be charitable purely to please a friend or to ensure I get some peace during my lunch break, that doesn't mean I don't want to do my bit. Hello, knitting for charity.

Here are some projects to get involved in:

- Knit tiny hats for bottles of Innocent smoothies to raise money for Help the Aged and Age Concern (www.innocentdrinks.co.uk/thebigknit)
- Knit squares to sew together to make a blanket for Macmillan's Comfort Blanket campaign (www.macmillan.org.uk/theknitter)
- Knit tiny clothes for premature babies who are too small to wear shop-bought clothes (http://preemiesuk.googlepages.com)
- Check out www.knittingforcharity.org or www.eparenting.co.uk/knit-fest/charityknitting.shtml for more ideas.

If you want to knit for charity but don't want to give up your slaved-over projects (and don't feel guilty about this), look no further than P/hop. P/hop (which stands for 'pennies per hour of pleasure') is a brilliant charitable endeavour that raises money for the emergency medical aid organization Médecins sans Frontières (Doctors Without Borders). Designers have donated knitting patterns for you to download free of charge from their website (www.p-hop.co.uk) and you are asked to make a small (or large, it's entirely up to you) donation based on how many hours of pleasure you anticipate getting from knitting the pattern. The sentiment behind this initiative is powerful – knitting gives me an enormous amount of pleasure and I am more than happy to give something back.

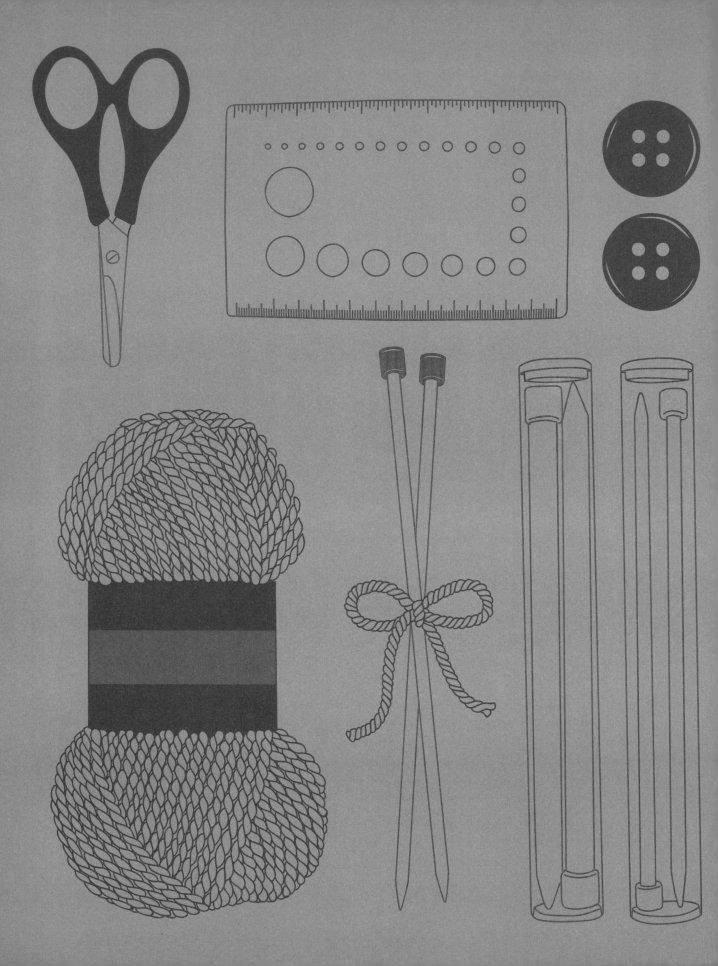

RESOURCES

Shopping

Here's a handy list of my favourite yarn shops, most of which offer an online service too.

London

All the Fun of the Fair (Unit 2, 8 Kingly Court, off Carnaby Street, London W1B 5PW, tel. 0207 287 2303, www.allthefunofthefair.biz): a delightful shop that sells everything you could need to knit plus a fantastic selection of vintage patterns, buttons and needles at very reasonable prices. They also run classes in the shop – check out their website for details.

I Knit (106 Lower Marsh, London SE1 7AB, tel. 0207 261 1338, www.iknit.org.uk): described as a sanctuary for knitters, this really is more of a knitting hub than just a shop. They run classes, have an active knitting group that anyone can join for free as well as a group for spinners and dyers and they host lots of fun events, including the brilliant I Knit Weekender (see p. 186). The best thing about this shop is their huge range of books (this is where I picked up my precious copy of Barbara Walker's *A Treasury of Knitting Patterns* series – see p. 109).

John Lewis (Oxford Street, London W1A 1EX, tel. 0207 629 7711, www.johnlewis.com): the haberdashery section gets packed at the weekends and the staff can sometimes be too harassed to give you a helping hand, but they stock a wide range of yarns, books, needles and knitting kits.

Liberty (Regent Street, London W1B 5AH, tel. 0207 734 1234, www.liberty.co.uk): this luxury department store has a wonderful haberdashery section that stocks the full range of Rowan yarns and lots of books and patterns. They also run classes and have a famous knitting group. The ladies who work in this section are so helpful – I heart Liberty.

Loop (41 Cross Street, London N1 2BB, tel. 0207 288 1160, www.loopknitting.com): a lovely cosy yarn shop that stocks a wonderful range of luxury yarns and needles. They also sell lots of Clover products (hallelujah!) and run classes too.

Peter Jones (Sloane Square, London SW1W 8EL, tel. 0207 730 3434, www.peterjones.co.uk): a part of the John Lewis group with a similar range of yarns, books, needles and kits.

Prick Your Finger (260 Globe Road, London E2 0JD, tel. 0208 981 2560, www.prickyourfinger.com): my local yarn shop, run by Rachael Matthews (see p. 25) and her friend

Louise. They stock a small but perfectly formed range of yarns, needles, buttons and books. Rachael's own quirky patterns are for sale too.

Sharp Works (236B Railton Road, London SE24 0JT, tel. 0207 738 7668, www.sharpworks.co.uk): run by mother – daughter team Susan Sharp and Rose Sharp Jones, they stock a nice range of yarns, books and patterns, run classes and have a knitting group.

Stash Yarns (213 Upper Richmond Road, London SW15 6SQ, tel. 0208 246 6666, www.stashyarns.co.uk): yarns, needles, books, patterns, classes and, intriguingly, yarn-tasting evenings.

Outside London

Here is just a small selection of the shops I know to be more than satisfactory:

Baa Ram Ewe (87 Otley Road, Headingly, Leeds LS6 3PS, tel. 0113 278 1788, www.baaramewe.co.uk)

Button and Skein (17 Church Street, off Market Square, Macclesfield, Cheshire SK11 6ET, tel. 01625 428608, www.buttonandskein.co.uk)

Cocoon (10 George Street, Hove, Brighton BN3 3YA, tel. 01273 776176, www.cocoonknits.co.uk)

Fiddlesticks (17 New Street, Honiton, Devon EX14 1HA, tel. 01404 47676, www.fiddlesticksdevon.co.uk)

Get Knitted (39 Brislington Hill, Brislington, Bristol BS4 5BE, tel. 0117 300 5211, www.getknitted.com)

John Lewis (stores nationwide, www.johnlewis.com); unfortunately, not all John Lewis stores have a haberdashery so phone ahead before making a visit.

K1 Yarns (136 Queen Margaret Drive, Glasgow G20 8NY; tel. 0141 576 0113, and 89 West Bow, Edinburgh, tel. 0131 226 7472, www.k1yarns.com)

Norfolk Yarn (288 Aylsham Road, Hellesdon, Norwich NR3 2RG, tel. 01603 417001, www.norfolkyarn.co.uk)

Yarn (55 Chilwell Road, Beeston, Nottingham NG9 1EN, tel. 0115 925 3606, www.yarn-in-notts.co.uk)

Yarn Over (The Labyrinth, Mark Lane, Eastbourne BN21 4RJ, tel. 01323 301153, www.yarnover.org.uk)

Online

There are a million and one places to buy yarn on the internet, from huge online megastores to tiny independent sellers who spin and dye their own yarn. Here are my tried and tested favourites:

Angel Yarns (www.angelyarns.com): claim to be Europe's largest online yarn store; they have a humungous range of yarns, books, needles and accessories and an active forum.

Etsy (www.etsy.com): a general craft website where individuals from all over the world sell their handmade goods, vintage wears and crafting supplies (including patterns). If you're after stunning and completely unique yarns from independent spinners and dyers, Etsy is the site for you.

First4Yarns (www.first4yarns.co.uk): the wonderful shop who satisfied my Malabrigo craving; they offer free delivery on orders over £10.

Laughing Hens (www.laughinghens.com): another large online store, these guys aim more towards the older knitter but have a great range nonetheless.

McA Direct (www.mcadirect.com): less focused on the luxury end of the market, and the yarns aren't as pretty, but they offer a great service with free delivery on orders over £10.

Pickles (http://shop.pickles.no): a small but growing selection of luxury yarns in colours that evoke the Scandinavian spirit of the two girls who run it.

Purl Soho (www.purlsoho.com): the online store of the best knitting shop in the world (Purl Soho in New York – if you're ever in the city, you *must* check it out. *Amazing*!). Purl stock an unrivalled range of utterly divine yarns and their international shipping costs are more than affordable.

Rowan (www.knitrowan.co.uk): Rowan = British yarn, as far as I'm concerned. You can't buy their yarns directly from this site but you can browse the full range and download free patterns.

Skein Queen (www.skeinqueenshop.co.uk): independent seller Debbie Orr runs this lovely little online boutique; all her yarns (which she has christened with pleasing names like 'sumptuous' and 'bamboozle') are spun and dyed by her own fair hands and are luxury par excellence.

The Toft Alpaca Shop (www.thetoftalpacashop.co.uk): a very chic store selling only their own British-made alpaca products. If luxury eco-friendly yarns in completely natural tones are your bag, this is the shop for you. I covet every single one of their very stylish knitting kits.

Web of Wool (www.webofwool.co.uk): the only place you need to go for sock yarn – they have by far and away the largest and prettiest selection I've ever seen.

Yarnzilla: (www.yarnzilla.com): a US store that stock an astonishing range of yarns. Shipping will set you back a little more than Purl but the site is so damn cute, it's worth the extra couple of dollars.

Getting Help

Teaching yourself to knit from scratch using only the pictures and instructions in a book is no easy thing and we all need a helping hand sometimes. If you find yourself staring befuddled at any of the instructions in 'How to Knit' and you still don't get what I'm on about, don't sit there for hours hoping that it'll eventually somehow sink in; get out there and seek reinforcement.

Your Granny

If she's around, Granny really is best (unless it's my granny, who has a strange tendency to knit things inside out) – it's likely she's been knitting for yonks and has the experience (and patience) to help you out. If you aren't lucky enough to still have your granny around, steal someone else's. You're more than likely to have a neighbour or family friend who fits the bill.

Your Mates

You'd be surprised by just how many people are getting knitty with it these days and while they'll mostly be happy to reveal themselves on the web, you may not know that Sally who sits opposite you at work/ catches your commuter train/runs next to you on the treadmill is a dab hand. Ask around – people with the skills are usually more than happy to pass them on. Chances are Sally will be a member of a knitting group you could join too.

The Internet

Learning to knit, I discovered a rather alarming number of bored housewives who amuse themselves by posting instructional knitting videos on the internet. Search on YouTube, eHow or Videojug for visual instructions on learning specific techniques and stitches. The videos aren't of the best quality, and if you're anything like me you'll feel a little uneasy watching Sue show the world how to purl in her living room, but they can be useful if you've been stuck for days.

If you have a complicated question that isn't just about getting your head around a particular instruction, get yourself on the Ravelry forum (see p. 180). Within minutes, you'll be looking at a whole heap of suggestions from some generous and experienced knitters.

Classes

Most of the yarn shops listed above run classes for beginner knitters (and advanced ones too). Get yourself down to your local shop; if they don't hold classes there, the knowledgeable shop assistants will be able to point you in the right direction.

Index

Notes